Women, Sex & Desire

Praise for Elizabeth Davis' work and writing

"The

...of Childbirth; The Complete Book of
Pregnancy and Birth; and The Place of Birth

"Elizabeth Davis loves and respects women, and her work places childbearing where it belongs—in the strong and capable hands of mothers and midwives."

— The Boston Women's Health Book Collective
Authors of Our Bodies, Ourselves

"The elements of caring for and caring about women are so maturely thought out and articulated that I readily recommend the book."

— Mary V. Widhalm, C.N.M., M.S.
Director of Midwifery
Lincoln Medical and Mental Health Center, New York

About the Author

A renowned expert on women's issues, Elizabe...
midwife, women's health care speciali...
for the past 17 years. She i...
rights, and is widely s...
of openness a...
S...

...n Ac-
...s a degree in
...ersity and is certified
...dwives. She lives in Windsor,
...of three children.
...ooks include the classic *Heart and Hands: A*
...uide to Pregnancy and Birth; *Energetic Pregnancy*; and
...en's Intuition. She has also written *The Women's Wheel of Life*, forthcoming.

About the Illustrator

Susan Brooks, an artist and metalsmith, maintains a working studio in Berkeley, California. She can be contacted at P.O Box 9775, Berkeley CA 94709, (510) 845-2612.

Women, Sex

...Every Stage of Life

Elizabeth Davis

Alameda CA

HUNTER HOUSE INC., PUBLISHERS
P.O. Box 2914
Alameda CA 94501-0914

Library of Congress Cataloging-in-Publication Data

Davis, Elizabeth, 1950–
Women, sex and desire : understanding your sexuality at every stage of life /
Elizabeth Davis.
p. cm.
Published in Great Britain under title: Women's sexual cycles.
Includes index.
ISBN 0-89793-195-5 (cloth) : $22.95. — ISBN 0 89793-194-7 (pbk.) :
$12.95
1. Women—Sexual behavior. 2. Sex (Psychology) I. Davis, Elizabeth, 1950–
Women's sexual cycles. II. Title.
HQ29.D295 1995
306.7'082–dc 20   95–33256   CIP

Set in Goudy, Journal, and Zurich by 847 Communications, Alameda CA
Printed and bound by Data Reproduction Corporation, Rochester Hills, MI
Manufactured in the United States of America

9 8 7 6 5 4 3 2 1   First U.S. edition

Ordering Information

Trade bookstores and wholesalers in the U.S. and Canada, please contact

PUBLISHERS GROUP WEST
4065 Hollis, Box 8843, Emeryville CA 94608
Telephone 1-800-788-3123 or (510) 658-3453
Fax (510) 658-1834

College textbooks / course adoption orders
Please contact Hunter House at the address and phone number above.

Orders by individuals or organizations
Hunter House books are available through most bookstores
or can be ordered directly from the publisher by calling toll-free:

1-800-266-5592

Project Editor: Lisa E. Lee   *Production Manager:* Paul J. Frindt
Copy Editor: Mali Apple   *Proofreader:* Lara Thompson
Cover Design: Design Works   *Book Design:* Dian-Aziza Ooka
Cover & Interior Illustrations: Susan Brooks
Sales & Marketing: Corrine M. Sahli   *Publicity & Promotion:* Darcy Cohan
Scheduling & Administration: María Jesús Aguiló
Customer Support: Joshua Tabisaura
Order Fulfillment: A & A Quality Shipping Services
Publisher: Kiran S. Rana

Contents

Foreword

by Germaine Greer

swelled, bur..
sciousness of real women outrag.. ..
demands made upon them. The struggle to vomit up th.. ...
ized guilt's and the ingrained certainties of defect and inadequacy
is not over, because male fantasy is still the deciding factor in our
buying and selling. The breast-popping stereotype still dangles her
four-foot legs off the car hood. The icon of the dazzling super-
menial whose hands never say housework, who is always accessible
to the penis and climaxes whenever her partner does (and is never
without a desirous partner), and never falters on the rope-bridge
over the chasm of parenting, is still displayed in all our houses. But
her stranglehold on female variety is gradually being loosened. Gay
women have defied her way up front. Heterosexual women too,
have steadily, quietly rewritten the agenda, to include singleness,
aging, aggression, wit, and sorrow. Character has been inscribed
upon the smooth featureless skin of the stereotype as women have
demanded the right to grow up and turn into people.

The great tension at the heart of feminism has always been
the pull to demand entry to the male world, and claim an equal
share of male characteristics, against the pressure for the right to
be different but not inferior. Some feminists argued for the indus-
trialization of motherhood and the right to carry arms in imperial-
ist wars and to direct the bone-crushing operations of
multinationals. Others wondered what real femaleness, as distinct
from prescribed femininity might be like. They moved into the

inscape of the gendered body, deconstructing biological femaleness not as defect, i.e. non-maleness, not as distortion of a male norm by the specific imperatives of child-bearing, but as a complex and variable norm in itself. They took to heart the biological lesson that it is not the female but the male that is the product of a defective gene.

A gifted and persistent group of women professionals set themselves the task of observing at first hand how female humans really do behave. They discovered that all kinds of received ideas about female anatomy were simply wrong, that all kinds of variation were contained within a normality far more capacious than anyone had realized before. Gradually the conviction that femaleness is a permanent disease began to lose its hold. Fathers rose from attending birthing women with a new respect for their resilience and power. Women turned away from the hospital and the clinic, looking for ways to take responsibility for their own well-being. Feminist observers put together a picture of a hitherto unknown creature, the well woman.

We still have a long way to go; the medical establishment still labors under the delusion that femaleness is a condition that demands treatment, that women's fertility is the cause of overpopulation, that machines are better at birthing than women, that wombs are something that should be extirpated, and that the menstrual cycle involves periodic insanity.

Elizabeth Davis has given women the kind of patient, loving, and respectful attention that is usually reserved for rhinos and mountain gorillas. Here is a practitioner who does not prescribe but describe, in terms that are both empowering and fascinating, the extraordinary inventiveness and variety of the human female in all her moods and phases.

Author's Note

nother book on sex, you say? What more can be said
~~~~ ~~~~~~~? Well, when it comes to sheer tech-

WOIK as a ~~~~~~~ ,
tor. I have been a midwife for 17 years, and have proviueu wen
woman gynecology and contraceptive care since 1980. I also ran a
study through the American Food and Drug Administration on
the cervical cap, a newly approved contraceptive device that has
been used throughout Europe for many years.

Although it was not the express intent of my research, use of
the cervical cap often prompted my subjects to raise issues regarding
their sexuality. In fact, many women chose to use the cap because
other methods had negative effects on sexual enjoyment. Others
found that in using the cap, they became more aware of their
anatomy than ever before and had questions about normal physiological changes during the monthly cycle and how these affect
sexual activity. Some of these questions were very basic, and it
became clear as I heard them time and again how little even the
most sophisticated women may know about hormonal cause and
effect when it comes to sexuality. Other issues raised were more
involved, regarding fluctuations of desire and emotional responses
under a variety of extenuating circumstances. It dawned on me
that bits and pieces of information—particularly physical details
alone—were not sufficient to meet women's needs. An overview of
women's sexuality that incorporated hormonal influences, natural
phases of desire during childbearing and rearing, and effects of

menopause, as well as the impact of stress, grief, and relationship upheavals was very much in demand. Thus *Women, Sex & Desire* was born.

Additional insight and data have been gleaned from my work as a midwife. Many people in this society have the idea that midwives only deliver babies. Not only does our scope of practice include women's general health, but it incorporates a large measure of patient education and counseling. Pregnancy, birth, and postpartum are very vulnerable times for women, times of rapid and often drastic change and adjustment. A woman's relationships with herself, her partner, and her close family and friends are brought up for scrutiny; a natural step, really, in preparing for parenthood. But as women feel uncertain in their changing identities, so too their partners may feel displaced, and marriage or family counseling becomes yet another aspect of caring.

Thus I have been privy to the confidences and confessions of hundreds of women in the childbearing cycle. I have also witnessed a fair amount of uninhibited sexual expression and response during labor itself. Although we are taught in this culture that birth is primarily a physical, medical event, in reality it is strongly psychosexual. The positions women take, the movements and sounds they spontaneously make during labor (when they feel free and safe enough to do so) are very similar to those in passionate lovemaking. An inextricable part of childbirth preparation is learning to let go completely, to trust one's body, its rhythms and instincts. Naturally, sexual awareness and expression are part of the picture.

Midwives also provide advice on nutrition, exercise, stress reduction, and lifestyle modifications conducive to health. Midwifery care is preventive care, aimed at promoting natural birth. Perhaps a bit of background is in order here: the word midwife comes from Old English and literally means "with woman." Midwifery has been a well established maternity care option in Europe for centuries, but is only now experiencing a resurgence in the United States. In the Netherlands, for example, midwives assist nearly 75 percent of all births, and over a third take place at home. The safety of midwifery care is demonstrated by the fact that the Dutch have one of the lowest perinatal mortality rates in the world, while the United States ranks a disgraceful 22nd.[1] Largely, this is due to inadequate prenatal care. But now, American women are beginning to seek out midwifery care for the humanistic, personalized approach missing from standard obstetrical care.

...... that labor

checkup, a woman tells me she has never had ... ... gentle examination, nor have her questions been answered so thoroughly and respectfully. I feel very grateful for my training and recognize its value. Midwifery has also been a way for me to learn about my own capabilities; as I have learned to trust myself, I have learned to trust women in general. Whenever there is a problem, I believe the woman herself can find the answer, provided she is given adequate information and support. I have discovered that in labor, women often know better than I how to advance the birth. I believe in women's strength and resourcefulness; I've witnessed it time and again. And I also believe that women have been severely shortchanged in a culture that defines them as either Madonna or whore. Women care about the continuation and continuity of life; they are intrigued by relationships, how things fit together. *Women, Sex & Desire* is an attempt to honor these attributes of women by presenting an overview in which the sexual aspect is not separated from everything else.

The first-hand accounts included in the text are paraphrases of comments made by my clients over the years and recent interview responses solicited through my women's health practice at Woman-to-Woman Clinic, San Francisco, California. May you be as moved and delighted by the candor of these comments as I have been, and may you draw from them—and the women who have shared them—the inspiration to understand, accept, and empower yourself!

Elizabeth Davis
Windsor, California 1994

1. Wagner, Marsden G., "Infant Mortality in Europe: Implications for the United States," WHO *Journal for Public Policy* (1988).

Women, Sex
& Desire

Chapter 1

If time and again you have been puzzled by your sexual mood swings, your whims, fantasies, and aversions, this book is for you! Women in civilized society have increasingly lost touch with their natural rhythms of sexual desire, particularly in cultures dominated by masculine values and attitudes. Virtually our only popular reference to female sexual rhythms is a negative one, pertaining to the unavailability or undesirability of menstruating women. This is a taboo that we will explore at length later, along with others regarding pregnancy, menopause, and sex in later years. But let us return to the issue at hand: what is the true nature of women's sexuality and women's sexual power?

Before we can even begin to answer this question, we must consider how culture has conditioned us to view sexuality in general. Ours is a black-and-white society; we are not too fond of shades of gray. The reason for this can be traced to our most fundamental religious ideology, Puritanism. This doctrine sees only good and bad, heaven and hell, God and the devil, devoid even of the intermediate states (purgatory) and figures (saints) of Catholicism and other orthodox religions. This simplistic theology carries over to our social life and institutions. Watch television any night of the week and you will see good characters and bad ones, with little in between. For years, American movies have featured heroic figures notable for their lack of complexity. This has changed somewhat, particularly with the input of women screenwriters and directors. Nevertheless, to escape our usual two-dimensional reality, we must sift through overt and covert sexual messages that constantly bombard and surround us.

Think about the myths you assimilated in childhood, particularly if you are of the baby-boom generation. Women are virtuous, men are scoundrels. Women don't want sex as much as men do, but they ultimately submit for security's sake. Woman's role is to tame and subdue man, generally by trickery and deceit. Man's role is to take charge, have all the fun and all the say, though laughable and foolish he may be.

Not much of a sexual-social legacy, is it? These suppositions are dehumanizing and demeaning to both sexes. They reiterate our cultural dualism via a definition of sexuality whereby men and women are mutually exclusive opposites. The advertising industry has never stopped sending the message that sex is a battleground. Men win by domination; women, by seduction and submission. Sure, women can have spunk, or a chip on the shoulder now and then, but their power and intelligence must not overshadow men's.

Our social values regarding sex are further expressed by language. Many slang words used to describe the sex act are distinctly unpleasant to women because they portray sex as an act of aggression, male upon female. What's more, these words all imply that sex equals penetration, and thus that the penis and vagina are the primary sex organs. There are few slang words for women's sexual organs anyway, but none in common use for the clitoris. This key source of female sexual pleasure and response is often left undrawn or unlabeled on anatomical sketches; a woman learns the word clitoris much later than a boy learns the word for his penis. And in sexual activity, male response is the standard against which female response is evaluated and judged. When the penis is suffused with blood, we call it erect, but the clitoris is said to be congested. Even the term vagina comes from the Latin for sheath or scabbard, suggesting a waiting and passive receptacle for the penis. As Sheila Kitzinger, authority on childbirth and women's sexuality, astutely observes, "language is either silent about women's bodies and sexuality or condemns them."[1]

And all of this lives on despite the sexual revolution. What was that all about, anyway? Technology was a major factor; the pill created new possibilities for sexual experimentation, and abortion became more readily available. Never before had young people ⸱ ⸱ ⸱ ⸱ ⸱ ⸱ ⸱ ⸱ ⸱ 1960₀ Theirs

have sex freely without having to take responsibility; effect, in retrospect, was an even greater burden on women and their relationships. Now we know that sex does not necessarily engender intimacy and, if premature or ill advised, may even inhibit normal development. The sexual revolution freed women to have sex according to their passions, but if they chose to avoid it, they were labeled hung-up or even frigid. Social attitudes regarding male superiority and privilege remained the same, so that many women felt more enslaved by their sexuality than liberated to explore its true potential.

Today, when I listen to my daughter's favorite pop songs, I hear messages to the effect that she is expected to "put out" sexually, and handle the wild and irresponsible behavior of her man *plus* her own emotional responses. Doesn't sound much like liberation to me! She must also worry about sexually transmitted diseases, pregnancy, and economic dependency should she conceive. No wonder that more women are waiting to become sexually active these days and are taking the decision to have sex much more seriously.

Underlying the persistent polarization of the sexes is the disharmony of masculine and feminine energies within us. We all have forceful, aggressive, and coolly analytical qualities traditionally considered male, and likewise, vulnerable, sensitive, and spontaneous qualities traditionally considered female. As we begin to speak of getting in touch with both sides of ourselves, we must also question what makes men and women uniquely what they are.

In this regard, groundbreaking research began with the Masters and Johnson study in 1966, which revealed for the first time women's orgasmic potential and the importance of clitoral stimulation. Foreplay became a household word, and even though women often feel they don't get enough, at least they don't have to explain what it is to their partners. In fact, some authorities now take exception to the term itself, as it implies that anything short of penetration is merely preliminary and therefore less significant. However, women's need and desire for foreplay can serve as a focal point for closer examination of differences between the sexes. Most women say that although foreplay is important physically, the emotional aspects of being cared for are even more critical. When foreplay occurs in a spirit of love and tenderness, it enhances physical relaxation and focus. Without the emotional component, foreplay may be little more than an irritation. This brings to mind the classic dichotomy of male/female readiness for intimacy: men need to have sex in order to feel close, women need to feel close in order to have sex.

How much of this is cultural, how much biological? Certainly, as primary caretakers of society and its offspring, women need support, particularly in caring for the very young. In our society, the trappings of security have traditionally been provided by men. But in other times, in pre-Christian matriarchal cultures, women cared collectively for one another and the children. Although men made important contributions to the system, women did not rely on them for support. These were agrarian societies, based on collective ownership of land and cooperative agricultural efforts. Women were central to these efforts, as well as those of child rearing and education, and depended primarily on the support of other women. Men played secondary roles, relationships were polyandrous, and women did not necessarily know who fathered their children. In fact, in many of these cultures men were not recognized as integral to conception, which was thought to take place by virtue of a woman's relationship with the spirit world. Notably, these were cultures of peace, with shrines and altars everywhere.[2]

Even where hunting was essential, women were originally at the center of things, clearly recognizable as givers and originators of life. Each person's loyalty was to his or her mother's clan, his or her sister's children. It took many thousands of years for men ⋅

⸻ ⸻ up to medieval times, particularly as healers and midwives, were tortured and burned at the stake in great numbers.[4]

No one really knows what female sexuality was like before cultural oppression, but we can speculate. The missionary position was probably not first choice; perhaps women straddled their partners, controlling the rate and depth of penetration, generating their own foreplay. According to ancient Tantric tradition (one highly reverent of women), the posture of choice was entwined sitting, which allowed a slow, steady buildup of passion that could at the same time be controlled and maintained.

In any case, today we have a complex situation in which traditional male dominance has been challenged by social upheaval. Women who were once expected to stay at home and care for their families have moved fully into the workforce, and many have been disillusioned by the stress and strain of trying to juggle multiple roles of mother, lover, homemaker, and executive. Unfortunately, our society has adjusted to the two-income family, so that giving up work or cutting back hours is economically impossible for many couples. It would seem that women are once again trapped, doomed to overwork or to dependency on men.

Except that men, too, are eager for change. This is the new generation of fathers who have comforted crying babies in the night, changed diapers, and altered their work schedules to take care of sick children. Having done so, these fathers have found the fast track not so glittery and far from gold, and many of them want to jump off. Recently, a major American newspaper ran results of a poll indicating that, given the choice, nearly 70 percent of women and 40 percent of men would cut back work hours to spend more time with their families. Woven into all of this is an increased awareness of the life cycle, ebb-and-flow patterns of rest and productivity, emotional ups and downs, creative spurts and periods of dormancy. Despite media messages to the contrary, neither women nor men are always active, nor should they try to be. It is no accident that our society is plagued with stress-related illnesses such as heart disease, high blood pressure, and eating disorders. The need for passing reflection, time off to appreciate life and one's own unique purpose, now touches both sexes.

How does all of this relate to sexuality? It is increasingly clear that sexual mores too are in upheaval, that the stereotypical roles of man as the aggressive provider and woman as the passive caretaker are outmoded. As new definitions of male and female needs and desires are forged in the United States, even the most entrenched and repressive cultures of the Middle East feel the winds of change. The European view of sexuality has long been unique for its incorporation of sensuality and emotionality while at the same time maintaining a strict double standard. This, too, is changing.

I recently saw a pregnancy and birth video that was produced in the Netherlands and was struck by the unusual opening sequence. This was actually a prolonged shot of a couple cuddling in bed in the morning, he with his eyes closed, a smile on his face; she talking a bit and nuzzling against his cheek. But this was not an afterglow scene; it was the tender moment when she first broke the news that she was pregnant. What struck me most was that here were two equals, vulnerable and strong, sensitive, in touch with themselves, relaxed and communicative. To her news he responded positively, maturely, with none of that feigned idiot shock the American male usually expresses upon hearing that he is going to be a father. This may be due in large part to the fact that Holland provides both maternity and paternity leave, home nursing and housekeeping care after the baby comes, and generous support, both social and financial, for the developing family.

Traditionally, the European view of extramarital sex has also been much more liberal than the American attitude. Again, we may look to Puritanical mores, the duality of mind and body (mind is good, body is bad) ~~ ~ ~

..~ grievous mistake of commingling with the serpent. New Age interpretations of this story see the serpent as Kundalini, or the vital power that may be awakened by uniting one's physical, sexual self with higher intelligence. My favorite T-shirt message sums it up very nicely: "Eve Chose Consciousness." But Christianity categorically maintains that to seek enlightenment through the body is tantamount to sin. What does this mean for women, who have no choice but to unite with their bodies in birth, or suffer? What does this mean for all of us but isolation, disease, and neurosis? To quote Susan Griffin:

> Consciousness and meaning are part of nature . . . . When bodily knowledge and language are separated, we ourselves experience a terrible separation which ranges all the way from grief to despair to madness . . . . In this way culture destroys a woman's conscious knowledge of her own experience. Just as she is separated from other women, from her body and her feelings, she is, finally, a stranger to herself.[5]

Fortunately, we have countered with feminism, at first intensely political but more recently humanistic, even spiritual. Against all odds, women are rediscovering their natural strengths, their unique abilities and propensities apart from men. They are pulling together in groups, purging themselves of mistrust and competitiveness. They are formulating communications systems according to need, devising social structures to support them in various life phases, reanimating ritual celebrations and acknowledgments from the past, or inventing new ones to suit the present. The new feminism, highly personal hence imminently practical, has evolved from our need to unite mind and body, to reclaim the psychosexual events of menstruation, childbirth, breastfeeding, and menopause as self-affirming and significant, rather than sinful or unclean, to derive power from being *female*.

Beyond simply acknowledging that our sexuality depends on our moods, and that these fluctuate according to hormonal, biological, and social influences, lies the potential to work with our rhythms instead of against them, to stop denying the ebb-and-flow patterns of existence and start using them to enhance the quality of our lives, not only for ourselves but for our loved ones, our culture, our world. It might well be said that to do so is crucial to our very survival. To my mind, woman's reunion with her body is a metaphor for healing the planet, saving the earth.

Accordingly, we must expand our definition of sexuality to reflect the interrelatedness of all life. We are accustomed to thinking of sexuality in the most limited way, as the physical act of intercourse alone. A more meaningful and pertinent definition is so broad as to be nearly unrecognizable: for a woman, sexuality is all that it means to be female. This may include physical, erotic expression, but it definitely involves the relationship of our vital energies to all aspects of existence. Actually, Webster's definition is not far off the mark: "The sum of structural, functional and behavioral peculiarities of living beings that subserve reproduction and distinguish males from females."[6]

Apart from cultural influences, then, are there behavioral differences between the sexes that can be linked to basic biology? While researching *Women's Intuition*,[7] I found that certain gender-specific characteristics reveal themselves early in infancy, long before acculturation takes place. For example, baby boys demonstrate a much stronger attraction toward tangible objects than do girls. Girls are more interested in the human face, in communication. Whereas men can see better in bright light and at a distance, women literally see the big picture: they have wider peripheral vision due to extra rods and cones at the back of the retina. And when it comes to tactile sensitivity, even the least sensitive woman is more sensitive than the most sensitive man (this is one test area in which scores of each ~~~ ˡ ˑ

˒ ˒˒˒˒ ˒˒ ˒˒˒ male superiority. But the current debate among leading female thinkers underscores the need for this information.

In her book *Backlash: The Undeclared War Against American Women*, Susan Faludi documents the myriad ways in which data have been misrepresented to undermine and subvert women's gains of the 1970s and 1980s, perpetuating, to some extent, feminism that sees men as the problem or at the very least calls for a change in male values and behavior. Camille Paglia, controversial author of *Sexual Personae*, finds this sort of feminism self-indulgent and simplistic, loaded with unrealistic expectations of what men must do in order for women to find true equality. "Women will never know who they are until they let men be men,"[9] she tells us, at the same time deriding feminists as sniveling, whiny women who ought just to get on with their lives. But she fails to place feminism in sociohistorical context, to honor its accomplishments and forgive its excesses. Beyond this polarization, I believe the promise of female autonomy may be found in embracing the achievements of our past as we work for a future where women can really be women. Men are not the target, though culture may be to some degree, or perhaps we are just beginning to see how truly separate and different are the basic natures of each sex.

To return to the research: we now know that the fetus itself produces hormones around six weeks' gestation that differentiate the sex organs and further affect brain development. The male cortex thickens on the right side; the female, on the left. The cortex contains key control centers that govern behavior; in the male functions are highly specialized according to hemisphere, but in the female functions are diffused, replicated on left and right sides of the brain. An outstanding example regards the emotional centers, which in women are located in both hemispheres but in men are found on the right side only. Add to the picture the fact that men have verbal centers only in the left hemisphere, and we see a biological basis for the difficulty men have in expressing their feelings.[10]

Due to a thickening of the corpus callosum (the part of the brain that connects the two hemispheres), women also show a much greater ability to switch back and forth between hemispheres. This may explain the female ability to coordinate several activities simultaneously, whereas males prefer to concentrate on one thing at a time. Women's attention is generally more diffused; their approach to problem solving is to encircle, consider the problem from a variety of angles, and then come to a conclusion. Men tend to be intensely focused in their problem solving, building in factors bricklayer-style, somewhat methodically. This is why, when the two sexes solve problems together, men are at a loss to understand why women bring in so many seemingly unrelated subjects and don't get to the point, while women wonder what's wrong with figuring things out by thorough discussion. Women by nature tend to expand, while men contract.

We can readily extrapolate these characteristics to differing sexual styles. John Gray, Ph.D., author of *Men, Women and Relationships*, notes that widespread misunderstanding of basic differences between the sexes is at the root of most sexual dissatisfaction and dysfunction.[11] What, then, does a woman need from a lover? Assistance in focusing, in bringing her diffused and expanded awareness (especially after a busy day) to focus on herself, her body, and sexual pleasure. It has been shown that women need an average of 18 minutes of stimulation to reach orgasm, whereas men need only two or three. Women need cuddling, they need to be held and touched in a nonsexual way at first, erogenous zones aside. As Gray astutely observes, the delicious, total-body pleasure a woman feels from this warm-up is much like what a man feels *after* his climax. A man will increasingly focus and contract his sexual tension until he ejaculates. Women and men can help each other by recognizing and balancing ...

... of emotional reactions and opportunities for self-expression. There is return and repetition but with continued growth, in a pattern resembling a spiral. Biological rhythms give women's lives meaning; they are vehicles for transformation. Every time a woman nears menstruation she will likely reflect on emotional difficulties and dissatisfactions in her life and have another go at their resolution. Menstruation occurs generally by lunar month, so that women are naturally tied to cosmic rhythms that profoundly influence existence.

Yet all of this may be negatively affected by the concept of woman as nurturer. Although this capability is to some degree biologically programmed, it has nonetheless been exploited by society. Remember that in a patriarchal system such as ours, woman as man's subordinate is responsible to him before herself. Despite clear evidence of hormonal and physiological factors in maternal instinct and behavior, there is no indication that this applies to the care of grown men, let alone those outside one's immediate family. And yet, for many generations women have been made to live their lives through others. Their worth has been assessed on the basis of how well they have fostered male "superiors": "Behind every good man there's a good woman." If or when the family falters, the guilt and blame invariably fall on the woman. She is responsible for discerning problems, implementing solutions, and coordinating everything to ultimate harmony. Predictably, she is so busy with these tasks that she seldom has time for herself. And how is she expected to respond to all this? She is to be long-suffering, self-sacrificing, stoic, faithful, complacent to life's "realities," yet willing and able to fight fiercely to defend her kin. Though a ludicrous image to many of us today, the social construct persists.

As we nurture others to the exclusion of ourselves, it follows that we will attempt to live out our dreams and fantasies through them as well. As the contemporary saying goes, "Women marry hoping to change their partners; men marry hoping their partners will never change." We must, once and for all, see this for what it is: a recipe for loss and disappointment. Only by asserting ourselves, by establishing our own needs and finding ways to meet them, can we hope to find fulfillment in life. Although we may want to nurture and care for others to a certain extent, let it be by choice rather than by obligation.

All things considered, it's hardly surprising that although women today are better educated and more socially sophisticated than at any time in recent history, we remain puzzled by and at the mercy of our hormonal and biological rhythms, unable to incorporate them successfully into our lives. This is largely because, as was stated earlier, our rhythmic energies engender an ebb-and-flow approach to living distinctly at odds with the masculine "ladder of success" model. But now perhaps we can begin to share with our partners and society a fuller definition of what it means to be a woman. These are the things women know: that everything comes around, that reflection is germane to creative action, and that the passage of time alone can be a key factor in change. We have learned these things organically, through the monthly cycle, in gestating young, in weathering the phases of childbearing and child rearing, in transforming through menopause. As society cries out for balance, for genuine solutions to overemphasis of the masculine, the unchecked pursuits of war and aggression at the cost of social services and education, women's wisdom is once again coming to the fore. Women are speaking out and being heard.

1. Sheila Kitzinger, *Woman's Experiences of Sex* (New York: Penguin Books, 1985).

2. Hallie Iglehart, *Woman Spirit* (San Francisco: Harper and Row, 1983).

3. Barbara Walker, *The Crone* (San Francisco: Harper and Row, 1985).

4. Barbara Ehrenreich ₋₋₄ ₙ ₋₋ ₋

7. Elizabeth Davis, *Women's Intuition*, (Berkeley, Calif.: Celestial Arts, 1990).

8. Anne Moir and David Jessel, *Brain Sex* (New York: Carol Publishing Group, 1991).

9. Camille Paglia, "Hurricane Camille Wreaks Havoc," *San Francisco Chronicle* (Sept. 1992).

10. Moir and Jessel, *Brain Sex*.

11. John Gray, *Men, Women and Relationships: Making Peace with the Opposite Sex* (Portland, Or.: Beyond Words Publishing, 1990).

2

Hormonal I-.Γ1

.... une animal kingdom
............iaii, at least) be omitted from the most highly evolved
species? I was familiar with the theory that women can and will
have sex at any time of the month, at any point in the cycle, due
to the intellectual aspect of human desire. Yet this was not a
fully satisfactory answer, for although it acknowledged the psy-
cho-logical component of women's desire it did not address the
physical and hormonal underpinnings, of which I knew virtually
nothing.

Later, after the birth of my second child, and after having
tried nearly every available type of contraception with varying de-
grees of dissatisfaction, I decided to learn about fertility awareness.
I soon discovered the postpartum period to be one of the most
challenging times to use this method, as I was still breastfeeding
and not yet menstruating, and was experiencing extreme hormonal
fluctuations. Yet, after some months of observation, I began to
catch on. Once I reestablished my normal cycle, I observed not
only the signs and symptoms of my fertility in mucus changes and
temperature fluctuations, but the emotional and sexual mood
swings that accompanied them. Beyond a doubt, I noticed that my
desire for sex was greater when I was fertile. What's more, I exuded
a copious vaginal secretion with a definite odor that seemed to put

both me and my partner in the mood. Perhaps, I thought, we women have a "heat" of our own after all!

I recently attended a midwifery conference. One of the few male presenters, a physician, mentioned in passing that according to his patients, the ovulatory phase was the time they felt most like making love. "How about the *only* time!" one of the women in the audience piped up, and the entire room broke into laughter. A moment of truth, it seems, and in marked contrast to the "any-time, ever ready" notion.

Let's look at the hormonal changes that occur day to day in the monthly cycle and examine how they influence sexual rhythms and response. But first, we must introduce the key hormones and consider their specific actions in detail.

THE HORMONES

We will start with estrogen, often considered the quintessential female hormone. It is made by the ovaries, under signals from the pituitary gland, which is further regulated by the hypothalamus.

Estrogen plays a major role during puberty, causing breast development, changes in sweat glands to produce body odor, changes in the vagina and its secretions, and enlargement of the external genitals (labia and clitoris). In the mature woman, estrogen triggers ovulation, and during pregnancy is responsible for breast growth, vaginal and cervical changes, and uterine enlargement.

Progesterone is the other key hormone in women's lives. It also is produced by the ovaries, specifically by the disintegrated egg follicle known as the corpus luteum. It too plays a role in the monthly cycle; once ovulation has occurred, progesterone keeps the uterine lining growing and rich enough to nourish the embryo in the event of conception. During pregnancy, it reduces uterine irritability so the uterus will retain its contents, and eventually its manufacture is taken over by the placenta.

Now let's see how these hormones work in concert during an average cycle of 28 days. As menstruation begins on day 1, one of the pituitary hormones, follicle stimulating hormone (FSH), sends a message to the ovaries to start producing estrogen. Around day 5, estrogen is released into the bloodstream and returns to the pituitary gland. When estrogen reaches a certain level, the pituitary secretes less FSH and releases another hormone, luteinizing hormone (LH).

This brings us to midcycle, or day 14. Estrogen is at its peak and LH flows to the ovary to stimulate one of ripen and release ~~

THE MENSTRUAL CYCLE

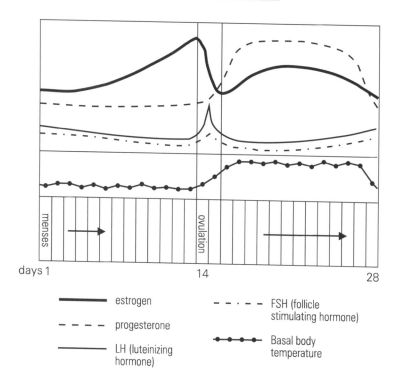

days 1   14   28

estrogen

- - - - progesterone

LH (luteinizing hormone)

- - - · - FSH (follicle stimulating hormone)

•-•-•- Basal body temperature

Progesterone reaches its peak around day 24 or 25; at this point, if fertilization has not occurred, LH shuts down, the corpus luteum withers, and progesterone levels drop sharply. Meanwhile, estrogen levels will have gradually reached their lowest point as well; when both have hit bottom, menstruation occurs.

Another hormone that fluctuates regularly in our bodies is testosterone, produced by the adrenal glands (as one of the family of androgens) and by the ovaries. Testosterone levels in women are seldom more than a tenth of that in most men, except during pregnancy if a woman is carrying a male fetus. In the monthly cycle, testosterone peaks twice a month, with ovulation and immediately before and during menstruation.

And then there is oxytocin, a hormone produced by the pituitary that is generated cyclically and in response to certain emotional stimuli. Oxytocin contracts the uterus and thus is naturally high immediately before and during menstruation. It has been found to enhance fertility in women by increasing movement of the fallopian tubes (and to increase the sperm count in men when given by nasal spray). More on this fascinating hormone in a moment.

PHYSICAL CHANGES
THROUGHOUT THE CYCLE

Now that the technical details are in place, let's consider the signs and signals we women experience at different points in the cycle. Keep in mind that the 28 day cycle is fairly common but far from standard; cycles may run as few as 21 days or more than 40. And month-to-month fluctuations are also normal.

Menstruation itself may last as few as three days or as many as seven. Women with longer periods often have a day in the middle when the flow stops, before a final day or two of bleeding. After menstruation there are usually several days with little or no vaginal secretion, known in the fertility-awareness method as dry days. (These are the days when, if you want to make love, you need ample stimulation to lubricate.) Depending on the length of menstruation and the overall length of the cycle, dry days may be numerous or entirely absent. How so? Take a look at the chart on page 28. This shows a comparison of several different women's cycles. Note that regardless of cycle length, ovulation occurs 14 days before menstruation begins. Barring abnormal conditions, this time span is biochemically fixed; room for variation occurs only in the pre-ovulatory phase, where length of menstruation, dry days, and pre-ovulatory days may be somewhat unpredictable in numb

...gers are pulled apart. This mucus has the same alkaline pH as seminal fluid and the perfect molecular structure for sperm to swim through. It can also keep sperm living in the vagina for a number of days. This is why, when using fertility awareness as a contraceptive method, you must abstain or use protection from the first sign of secretion after dry days. You never know when your mucus will shift to fertile, and as it does, any sperm in the canal or cervical crypts (small pockets within the cervical opening) can be kept viable until the egg is released.

Fertile mucus lasts approximately five to seven days, then shifts abruptly back to a drier, stickier, yellow-white discharge. However, a woman is not safe from pregnancy until three and a half of these post-ovulatory days have passed, allowing time for the more acidic pH of this mucus to kill off any remaining sperm. In a 28-day cycle, this brings us to about day 19 or 20.

The rest of the month is characterized by the same stickier mucus—with one exception. Just before menstruation begins, some women note a secretion that closely resembles fertile mucus. This is actually a mucus plug from the cervix, developed under the influence of progesterone, that protects the uterus from infection; it is shed spontaneously as progesterone levels fall. Now menstruation is set to begin.

SAMPLE MENSTRUAL CYCLES

Average/Long Cycle		Short Cycle		Stress-related Cycle	
Day	*Discharge*	*Day*	*Discharge*	*Day*	*Discharge*
1	menses	1	menses	1	menses
2	menses	2	menses	2	menses
3	menses	3	menses	3	menses
4	menses	4	spotting	4	spotting
5	menses	5	menses	5	dry
6	spotting	6	menses	6	dry
7	dry	7	spotting-slick	7	slippery
8	dry	8	slick	8	moist
9	dry	9	stretchy	9	moist
10	dry	10	dry	10	damp
11	dry	11	dry	11	dry
12	dry	12	dry	12	dry
13	creamy	13	dry	13	stretchy
14	creamy	14	dry	14	slippery
15	wet-milky	15	dry	15	wet
16	slippery	16	dry	16	dry
17	stretchy	17	gummy	17	dry
18	dry	18	gummy	18	dry
19	gummy	19	dry	19	pasty
20	dry	20	slippery	20	gummy
21	pasty	21	damp	21	dry
22	pasty	22	menses	22	dry
23	gummy			23	dry
24	dry			24	dry
25	dry			25	dry
26	dry			26	dry
27	dry			27	dry
28	damp-spotting			28	menses
29	slick				
30	menses				

An important aside: bear in mind that it takes time, usually at least six months of observation, to know enough about your cycle to be able to use contraception selectively. For example, fertile mucus looks very much like arousal lubrication, and cervical secretions may be severely altered by vaginal infection. You must allow enough time to incorporate such variations in your understanding.

Besides ch~~

~~ ~~om the ovary.

Breast and weight changes later in the cycle are partially due to a second, lesser peak of estrogen; they are further exaggerated by the presence of progesterone. Progesterone is known as a heat-producing hormone, and high levels may cause a noticeable rise in body temperature. In contrast, when levels plunge premenstrually, women typically experience cold hands and feet.

There are other physiological changes that account for the many premenstrual symptoms. High levels of androgens may cause intestinal cramping or diarrhea; conversely, some women experience constipation in this phase. Androgens also cause expansion and contraction of blood vessels; as levels fluctuate, women may experience headaches, inflammation of varicose veins, or rapid heartbeats.

A common question among women in their mid-thirties is why premenstrual syndrome seems to be getting worse, or if never a problem before, noticeable for the first time. As we mature, the midcycle estrogen peak soars higher, while the second rise tends to diminish. Thus there is less estrogen to modify effects of progesterone and androgens in the second half of the cycle. Very young women tend to experience similar effects but for different reasons—as their bodies are still maturing, adolescents have less estrogen to modify relatively high testosterone and androgen levels.

During menstruation, levels of progesterone and estrogen are at their lowest points (although the pituitary gland is primed to release FSH and set the cycle in motion once more). It is interesting that this hormonal low point is literally a fallow phase, a time free enough of hormonal influences for rest, reflection, and rejuvenation naturally to occur.

EMOTIONAL AND SEXUAL MOOD SWINGS

Perhaps you have already begun to link these physical changes to your own patterns of emotional and sexual response. As menstruation ends and dry days begin, it's no wonder that many women don't feel much like making love. After all, vaginal dryness isn't particularly erotic, and on a purely physical level, the hormonal upswing has just begun. However, many women find the pre-ovulatory phase a great time to make plans and, as estrogen and testosterone increase, a great time to get things done.

Accordingly, ovulation is the high point of the month, generally a time of peak performance. A fascinating study cited in a newspaper some years ago showed that women in their fertile phase scored higher on achievement tests than at any other time of the cycle, turning in top performances in athletic competitions, written examinations, and intelligence tests![1] The physical components of the fertile phase—elevated body temperature, fullness and sensitivity of the breasts, the slippery wetness of the vagina as though already aroused—often add a dimension of self-confidence, certainty, and richness to a woman's demeanor. All systems are "go"; when we are fertile, we're "on." And yes, like it or not, we are definitely "in heat"; were our genitals exposed and visible to potential partners (rather than being wiped dry repeatedly during the day or deodorized with pantyliners), telltale signs both visual and olfactory would signal our biological receptivity.

Women who are unaware of the cycle of mucus changes often think they are developing an infection during the fertile phase. It's not that the discharge is offensive, it's just that it is so profuse, and tends, when exposed to air and kept warm (as in underwear), to develop a rather musty odor. One woman graphically described this as a "barnyard smell": somewhat sweet and strong. As a matter of fact, women's sense of smell is more acute than men's, and around ovulation is especially attuned to a musklike odor associated with men (the synthetic form of which is called exaltolide). It is a smell most women find quite attractive.

Needless to say, this is a great time for lovemaking. As Sharon says, "It's the time . . ."

. . . that they feel decidedly amorous around this time. Sara describes it this way: "For me, there is both passion and tenderness. I really want Tom, but I don't feel tense or rushed about it. I feel ripe, full, with passion all through me. I feel like playing and taking my time, because I know my body is set for maximum sensation and incredible orgasm."

Women typically describe orgasms when fertile as "deep, very deep in my vagina," "at the core of my being," or "a total body experience." One woman went on to say, "I feel like my whole body, all of me, is one giant sexual receptor." Another states, "I feel sacred when I'm fertile, like all of me is at its best. I feel integrated, free."

Mary vividly describes not only her physical response but her emotional tone as, "Sweet . . . it's like waves of warm honey flowing through me." Another woman notes, "This is the time when I can really move a tremendous amount of energy through my body. Sometimes, other times when we make love and I come right away, I feel a little let down. But when I'm fertile, there's so much charge I can build it up, spread it out, and keep doing that until my orgasm is a total thing, it just carries me off completely." The qualities of "totality" and "sweetness" we can link to estrogen. The desire for sex, pure lust, is linked to the testosterone peak.

This discussion would not be complete without some mention of pheromones, olfactory stimulants released through the perspiration of both men and women. Winnifred B. Cutler made groundbreaking news in 1986 with her discovery that male pheromones could serve to regulate female menstrual cycles. With just a bit of pheromone substance (collected from male sweat samples) placed under their nostrils, 70 percent of women with highly irregular cycles became regular in a matter of months. Similarly, in 1971 Martha McClintock demonstrated the menstrual synchrony of women sharing quarters in college dorms, also due to the effects of pheromones. Even more intriguing is the finding that in monogamous couples, sexual rhythms tend to synchronize, with male testosterone surges matching female estrogen and progesterone, largely in response to pheromone exposure.[2]

And yet, beyond hormonal factors and physical cues there must be, for the intelligent, thinking creatures we women are, an element of desire that springs entirely from the awareness of our fertility and the knowledge that we have the power to conceive. Not necessarily the intent, but the power to re-create ourselves. Listen to what Ellen has to say: "Just knowing I'm fertile gets me completely turned on. This is the time of the month when I feel the power of creation flowing through me. Once my partner is aware, too, he intensifies my feelings with his own. We use condoms, and sometimes we 'play the edges' by having long, drawn-out foreplay, with an element of danger and excitement in being unprotected until we finally get the condom in place. The *charge* we build up, the intimacy, is really something else!"

The flip side of this is the difficulty some couples have in using contraception with this awareness, in the sense that it may feel like a violation or, at the very least, a letdown. Some choose to use fertility awareness as their only method of birth control and either abstain during ovulation or have sexual activity other than penile/vaginal intercourse.

Particularly if a couple has children already and thus knows the ultimate potential of this time, or if one wants another child while the other does not, the emotional content of sex during this

phase can be rather explosive. Ultimately, sex is a vehicle of communication, and as such does not always trigger easy or pleasant
revelations.

We will look more at contraceptive methods and issues later
in the chapter; suffice it for now to say that the fertile time is
indeed a power point. Apart from sexual activity, some women
actually plan key business meetings, important family events holi
days, or new vent...

... that the post-ovulatory phase is nothing
but a downhill slide? Not really, for although estrogen diminishes,
progesterone picks up. Nevertheless, there are other substances
released from the adrenals, called aldosterones, that apparently
have something of an opposite effect to that of the androgens.
Thus some women do report less sexual activity immediately after
ovulation.

Several days before menstruation, however, when progesterone levels are still high and androgens rise again, many women
notice a second sexual peak in the cycle. Asked to characterize it,
they say, "hot," "intense," "urgent," "driving," or "very physical."
Remember that progesterone is heat producing; it is interesting
how these sexual metaphors correspond to this quality. Samantha
says, "Right before my period, I feel, I don't know, more masculine
in my approach to sex, more aggressive." And from Joan, "I want
it fast, hot, physically rough . . . I come quickly, explosively—it's
great!" Ann observes, "I'm less emotional about sex—really, I just
want to get off."

Mild premenstrual symptoms such as heightened sensitivity
of the skin, especially the breasts and nipples, may further increase
sexual pleasure. Many women prefer being on top during lovemaking at this time so they can control the depth of penetration, the

angle, and the rate of clitoral stimulation. Plus, there is more opportunity in this position for being touched and caressed. On the other hand, if premenstrual symptoms are severe, it may be that *any* stimulation will be too much until menstruation is underway.

A few words about PMS in general: one theory is that low progesterone levels could be a cause. This may be your problem particularly if you experience breakthrough bleeding or spotting several days before your period begins (remember, progesterone's job is to maintain the uterine lining). In fact, increasing numbers of women in my practice are reporting this occurrence as periodic or even chronic. It's possible that progesterone levels are low relative to an excessive amount of estrogen taken through the diet via certain foods. The use of stilbestrol, an estrogen-like substance, is quite common for fattening beef cattle and for making the meat more tender. However, residues remain and become highly concentrated in milk and milk products. An obvious solution is to minimize consumption of these foods or look for natural alternatives. Another possibility is acupuncture, which can be used to stimulate the pituitary gland and subsequently the ovaries, to produce estrogen and progesterone in appropriate amounts.

The use of progesterone by ingestion or vaginal suppository has been randomly successful at best, and may have little more than a placebo effect for conditions other than that cited above. After all, it's the pituitary that masterminds ovarian function; it doesn't make sense that dosing the body with hormones would create any lasting effect. Recent studies have in fact shown that even women with severe PMS generally have normal amounts of estrogen and progesterone during the cycle. Another theory is that abnormal levels of serotonin in the brain may cause PMS and that the amino acid L-tryptophan may somehow be implicated in alleviating symptoms. L-tryptophan in excessive amounts can be dangerous, but certain foods, such as turkey, have naturally high amounts.

It is fairly easy to correlate emotional responses of moodiness, anger, borderline hysteria, and fear to hormonal shifts around menstruation. But beyond hormonal influences, might there not also be certain psychological precursors to PMS? I recall a client of mine who was quite concerned that she might be pregnant—she was two weeks late and had never missed a period, yet two pregnancy tests came back negative. Several days later she reported this dream: she was in her office, feeling under pressure due to a boom in her business, and her papers began blowing around, all over everywhere, when she heard a voice say, "just let go." As it turned out, she actually ~~~~ ¹

, ... the next. Before the sorting and reordering, dreaming and developing must come the release, the surrender, the death of the old. Consider again the hormonal influences: after progesterone peaks, both it and estrogen plummet—no gradual dip or decline, but rather, a harrowing fall. And testosterone, essentially a male hormone, may further spur us to ruthlessly reexamine hidden parts of ourselves, our direction in life, our significant relationships. Making way for the next cycle means getting out of the way intellectually, bottoming out, getting down to one's essence. This is the basis of renewal.

Depending on how readily or easily this occurs, sex may or may not seem desirable. As Sandra reports, "Once I know my period is going to start—I'm cramping or spotting a little—I like to wait on making love until it really gets going. I feel like keeping to myself until I've turned the corner. It's an energy thing for me." Quite the opposite, Pat reports, "A day or two before my period—wow, look out—I've got only one thing on my mind!"

Even if our premenstrual symptoms are relatively mild and consistent, all of us have a terrible time of it now and then. Screaming at our kids, fighting with our loved ones, breaking or throwing things, crying in public places—these extremes are usually the tail end of a very trying, difficult month, or perhaps a period of less than optimal health. Poor health and stress can definitely disrupt the metabolism and affect hormonal balance. Keeping tabs on ourselves day to day, not overdoing it, getting enough rest and relaxation all help, but sometimes circumstances go beyond that. Take a look at the box on page 37 for special ways to cope.

And now, one of the most persistent taboos: sex during menstruation. Even as little as five years ago, women were cautioned by physicians that it might lead to infection ("blood is a good culture medium for bacteria"), and many men are still influenced by ancient taboos that depict association with menstruating women as a brush with the dark side. Why so? Well, in biblical times a menstruating woman was considered unclean, as was everything she touched. Under the laws of Moses, sex was strictly forbidden during, and for a week after, the period. Since a woman's primary function at this time was to produce as many children as possible, it's likely her chances were intensified by staying away from her husband for a while so his sperm count could increase, then later reuniting with him right in midcycle.

Even in so-called primitive societies, women have long been isolated during menstruation, not for being unclean, but overly powerful and magical. The fact that women could bleed without consequence of illness, debility, or death was definitely confounding and frightening to the men of these cultures. However, in the matriarchies of ancient times, the menstrual phase was considered a time when women might unify earthly and heavenly influences. Heavenly, in that women seem linked to lunar forces as they tend to menstruate on new or full moons. Earthly, in that they embody cycles of birth, death, and rebirth found in nature; before the days of tampons or pads, women let themselves bleed into the earth, their blood revered as sacred.

In her wonderful book *Red Flower*, Dena Taylor documents a wide range of response to menstrual symptoms, featuring cross-cultural perspectives. Particularly noteworthy is the desire for seclusion; women speak of wanting to curl up in bed and relax, sleep by themselves, and avoid going out in public. Some speak of wanting

WAYS TO COPE WITH PMS

1. **Evoke your emotions**   Listen to the most sentimental, moving music you can find, the kind that hits the spot, and let yourself cry, yell, rave freely. As we midwives say to women postpartum, "letting the tears flow will let the milk come down"; the same is true of tears and menstruation.

2. **Experience the dark** ~~...~~

~~......~~ that as naturally as women gain a few pounds premenstrually, they lose them immediately afterward. In one study, the control group struggled to control food cravings. They didn't gain weight, but they didn't lose weight once menstruation was over, either! You *need* more calories at this time. Many women report cravings for milk products and green vegetables, which balance out the typical chocolate and sugar cravings that provide only a temporary lift.

5. **Exercise**   An all-over, aerobic routine is especially good. Aerobic exercise stimulates circulation and elimination, thus counteracting symptoms like bloating, cramping, and fatigue.

6. **Stay warm**   To compensate for circulatory disruptions, stay cozy. Wear socks, wrap up in a blanket, take a sauna, turn up the heat, and wear loose, comfortable clothing (forget the tight jeans).

7. **Make space for yourself**   Take time off, find ways to defer responsibilities, or duck out of them altogether if they really are excessive. Make time to be alone, to do things that make you feel good; in a word, indulge.

8. **Have sex if you want to**   A little sex goes a long way toward alleviating premenstrual tension. Be yourself—weepy, passionate, outrageous, outspoken—and make sex work for you. Masturbate, enjoy your body.

9. **Celebrate when your period begins**   Do some sort of letting-go-of-the-old ritual, burn letters, discard objects that symbolize entanglement, make affirmations of ending and new beginning.

to be only with women, and how nice it would be to have a special place (like a hut) where they could gather with others who were also menstruating.[3]

Ernest Hartmann, author of *The Biology of Dreaming*, notes that women dream most between days 25 and 30 of the cycle. These dreams are often sexual, sometimes violent and aggressive, as compared to dreams during ovulation, which are generally more soothing and somewhat passive. Specifically, dream images during menstruation include speaking animals, animals with men's heads, violent acts, and broken eggshells, whereas ovulating women report dreaming of babies, fragile things, jewels, eggs, and their mothers.[4] Women tend to dream about having sex with their partners or dear friends when ovulating; when menstruating, sex with strangers.

In fact, it is the premenstrual phase that is most noted for dreams of violence and death. This makes sense, really, as it is the lowest point hormonally and the turning point as well. I've found myself melancholy and wondering what I would do if one of my children died, or sometimes having feelings of inadequacy or despair over difficult situations in my life that I fear will never change. When I start flowing, my emotions loosen up and I become myself again. It is particularly interesting that PMS is apparently more severe when sleep is inadequate; Ernest Hartmann conjectures that perhaps women need more sleep at this time for the natural release of dreaming. (Note, however, that tranquilizers and sleeping pills sometimes prescribed for PMS may repress or inhibit dreaming.)

In the Native American tradition, some tribes believe that a girl's dreams at menarche (her first period) tell of her mission or direction in life. According to Brooke Medicine Eagle, Native American woman and shaman, the most prophetic dreams and visions of the future, including unimaginable events like the coming of the white man, were "brought to the people through the Moon Lodge," or women's ritual place of seclusion during menstruation.[5]

I have come to believe that the psychic propensity of women immediately before and during menstruation is primarily linked to

MOON PHASE ENERGIES AND MENSTRUATION

Waxing moon menstruation

The waxing moon is a time of growth, of new processes coming into play, and of new beginnings. This is a time to turn inward and to pay attention to one's own wisdom, as well as a time to learn new things and make discoveries.

In Native American culture, the animal of the waxing ~~~ · ·
~~~ · · · · ·

~~~ ·~~ ·~ a charged phase and a challenging one emotionally, when the dragon nature of menstruating women is fully evident.

The animal of the full moon, in Native American culture, is the phoenix, who burns to ashes and then rises anew, and the goddess is Ishtar, Red Goddess of Babylon.

Waning moon menstruation

The waning moon parallels sunset, a time when energy subsides and stabilizes. Now is the time to firm up plans, substantiate discoveries, verify knowledge, and let ideas bear fruit.

In Native American culture, the animal of this phase is the she-bear, who signifies the womb and is therefore productive. In ancient Greek culture, it is the goddess Demeter, who signifies the harvest.

New moon menstruation

The new moon is inwardly focused and the time for contemplation, reflection, germination. This is the midnight phase, also a time for rest and recuperation. Subconscious memories and anxieties rise to the surface; events are reviewed.

The animal of this phase is the toad: wise, slippery, solitary, and untouchable (due to her poisonous exterior). The goddess is Hecate, the crone, the reaper, the dark one.

Adapted from *Dragontime* by Luisa Francia (New York: Ash Tree Publishing, 1988).

the effects of the hormone oxytocin. As mentioned earlier, this hormone peaks during ovulation, another time women note great clarity and insight in their work and dealings with others. Oxytocin is an amazing hormone in that it is released not only under certain physiological conditions, but in response to emotional stimuli. For example, oxytocin causes vaginal lubrication and nipple erection when we think longingly of a lover or anticipate sexual contact. Breastfeeding mothers reminded of their baby by the cry of another often experience an oxytocin-based let-down of milk by mere thought alone. Similarly, a women overwhelmed with passion for her partner may have an orgasm the moment she is entered, with very little stimulation. No wonder oxytocin is called the "love hormone"! And it is released in even greater amounts with actual sexual activity such as caressing, kissing, breast stimulation, and orgasm.

Regarding the heightened awareness created by this hormone, women commonly report moments of creative inspiration with lovemaking or afterglow. In pregnancy, when oxytocin is at an all-time high, women speak intuitively of knowing their child before it is born, its nature and sex. As per menstruation, what society terms raving madness may actually be visionary insight, or at the very least, its potential. Menstruation affords us a cyclic opportunity to explore life's mysteries, and perhaps, with the right frame of mind and support, a chance to peer unflinchingly into the future.

If you are curious about your dreams at this point in your cycle but generally don't remember them, begin by keeping paper and pen by the bed. And be sure to record your recollections immediately upon awaking, even if it's four o'clock in the morning. Despite what you may think, you won't remember them later.

Not surprisingly, women often report yet another peak of sexual activity several days into the menstrual flow. For some, the first two or three days are unappealing due to general messiness, but as the flow shifts from heavy to moderate, passion picks up. Says Nancy, "Frankly, I like sex best when I'm having my period. I don't have to worry about pregnancy (I know my cycle) and I'm in a certain mood—feisty, steamy. I'm pre-lubricated too, and you know, I don't mind the blood all over everything: it's erotic to me and my partner." Or, as Jane says, "I feel free, I feel primal, I feel connected to my power. The blood turns me on: it's a symbol of life, the color of passion." And from Ana, "Actually, I think it's hormones, coming back around, picking up again. I know it's not the usual image, but I feel fresh, renewed. I don't think about the past. I think about the f ·   "

...ᴜᴏᴏ for many women regards whether or not conception is possible during menstruation. This was, in fact, one of the questions most often missed by the public on the recent (1990) Kinsey nationwide sex quiz. The correct answer is yes, although only rarely does this occur. In truth, the body does not menstruate and ovulate simultaneously, but the two can occur back to back. For example, a woman with a 21-day cycle might ovulate as early as day six or seven (remember that the post-ovulatory phase is fixed at 14 days). If she also has a five-day menstrual flow, there might already be mucus present on day 5 that could keep sperm viable until the egg is released a day or two later. Conception on days 1, 2, and 3 is virtually unheard of, particularly when the flow is heavy. Yet the fear of pregnancy may prevent women from enjoying the free days that do exist at this point and making the most of them.

And where does this bring us? Back to the beginning—we have come full circle on our hormonal journey. However, there are definite variations for women suffering from gynecological problems and illnesses, or for those under the influence of certain contraceptive methods.

HEALTH PROBLEMS
THAT AFFECT THE CYCLE

Failure to menstruate altogether is called amenorrhea. The condition may be caused by insufficient body fat, tumors of the hypothalamus or pituitary gland, thyroid disease, diseases affecting the central nervous system, diabetes or other chronic diseases, destruction of the endometrium (uterine lining) by excessive curettage (as used in D and C procedures or abortions), drug or alcohol addiction, adrenal disorders, ovarian cysts, or certain drugs. More often, a missed period is caused by stress, or by rigorous athletic training.

There are several diseases and conditions that so affect the cycle as to require in-depth examination. Endometriosis has become almost commonplace in recent years and is a major cause of infertility. Here is what happens: endometrial tissue somehow escapes from inside the uterus to implant itself on the outside of the pelvic organs, and proceeds to function as usual by going through cyclic changes. However, as there is no natural way for this tissue to be shed (as normally happens in menstruation), it will scar over repeatedly until adhesions (abnormal attachments between the pelvic structures) form. This may cause the uterus or tubes to twist, prevent eggs from being released, or lead to the development of ovarian cysts, which ultimately disrupt ovulation.

What causes endometriosis? Cutler has speculated that sex during menstruation may cause endometriosis. However, since her study population was extremely limited and no account was made of previous cervical or uterine trauma, her results are inconclusive at best.[9] A more popular theory is that a scarred or tightly closed cervix (due possibly to pelvic infection or traumatic abortion) may not allow a full release of the menses, which then passes out of the ends of the fallopian tubes and imbeds in adjacent pelvic tissues. Symptoms include abnormal bleeding, and pain with ovulation, menstruation, intercourse, or bowel movements. As mentioned earlier, infertility may be another symptom. However, pregnancy can cure the problem, since the natural hormonal changes of that process tend to shrink the implants almost completely. Sometimes birth control pills or other medications prove helpful, although alternative approaches such as acupuncture, homeopathy, and herbal treatments may work as well or better.

Yet another ailment known as polycystic ovarian disease (or Stein-Leventhal syndrome) causes serious hormonal imbalance: low FSH, high estrogen, erratic surges of LH, low progesterone, and elevated male hormones. The ~~~¹

                                    ..... cause the egg to break away. But this does not happen; instead the follicle cyst continues to enlarge. At worst, the cyst might rupture and cause internal bleeding. At the same time, high estrogen levels prevent the uterus from shedding so there are no menses, and this buildup of the endometrium increases the risk of uterine cancer.

How might a woman know she has polycystic disease? Often, the cyst will cause pain or discomfort in the pelvic region. She would notice significant changes in menstruation and might also observe abnormal growth of facial or body hair in response to elevated male hormones.

Yet another condition that drastically alters a woman's cycle is hysterectomy. Of course, if all the reproductive organs are removed, immediate menopause ensues. Sometimes, even if the uterus is diseased, the ovaries are fine and can be left in place so that normal hormonal production continues. For further information on complete hysterectomy, see Chapter 6.

Beyond these conditions, there are factors apt to affect the cycle of any woman living in typical contemporary fashion. Artificial lighting may disrupt the influences of moonlight and cause irregularities in the cycle, particularly if one lives in an area with a streetlight right outside the bedroom window. Opaque blinds can be

HERBS FOR MENSTRUATION

- **Basil** *(Ocimum bascilicum)*, particularly the fresh leaf, stimulates bleeding, invigorates, and lifts feelings of depression. A favorite way to take basil is by making pesto dishes; serving it with pasta is especially good, as the carbohydrates are stabilizing at the onset of menstruation.

- **Catnip** *(Nepeta cataria)* is pain killing, cramp easing, soothing, and calming. It is further renowned for its ability to ease colic in newborns.

- **Ginger** *(Zingiber officinale)* stimulates circulation, warms and balances the body, and helps dispel gastrointestinal upsets.

- **Life root** *(Senecio aureus)* can be taken by tincture: five to ten drops daily help regulate the cycle and ease PMS. It can also help relieve severe cramps, both uterine and intestinal. Herbal lore has it that life root blossoms were found carefully placed on the oldest grave known.[8] It is especially effective taken long-term.

- **Motherwort** *(Leonurus cardiaca)* is most effective by tincture: take ten drops to relax, fifteen drops to ease menstrual pain. Motherwort is also used for hot flashes during menopause and to ease labor pains.

- **Nettle** *(Urtica dioica)* helps get rid of excess water and reduce bloating, while strengthening the kidneys and adrenals. It also provides key minerals (such as calcium and iron) vitamin K, and carotene, and plenty of protein. It is especially useful for excessive bleeding.

- **Raspberry** *(Rubus species)* is said to represent women's passion and life force. Raspberry tea eases PMS and tones the uterus; it is mood-elevating and brings, according to Luisa Francia, "passionate menstruation." It is the beverage of choice for women throughout pregnancy and postpartum.

- **Rosemary** *(Rosmarinus officinalis)*, either oil or leaf, is strengthening and stabilizing to the body. It stimulates bleeding and helps keep energy high and consistent during menstruation.

With all herbs, source and processing make all the difference. Familiarize yourself with fresh herbs available in your area, and seek out distributors who carry organic products. Good tinctures are dated for reference and generally appear clear, not muddy.

used to reproduce more natural conditions of living out of doors; the blinds should be down completely around new moon time.

And then there is the busy pace of life, which is particularly grueling for a woman having to coordinate numerous activities. We all have daily, personal biorhythms: times throughout the day when we naturally seek out food, rest, or stimulation. Some women are morning types, some more nocturnal. Frequently, our personal rhythms are at odds with

⎯g, along with our impulses to socialize, create, or be solitary.

Fast-food, stimulants like coffee, sugar, and chocolate, and sedatives like alcohol all obscure our natural biorhythms. This doesn't mean we must give these up, but we do need to keep an eye on our intake. These substances tend to debilitate our bodies and place stress on our systems so that we lose vitamins and minerals and need to take supplements. Moreover, when we are less than healthy, our emotional reactions are extreme, our responses to various phases in the cycle become more exaggerated, and our abilities to rise to challenges day by day become impaired.

That our modern diet is also devoid of tonic and medicinal herbs is unfortunate, but this is something we can work to change. Herbs are allies to health and harmony; when one starts using herbs for self-improvement, desires for harmful substances or less-than-healthful foods often begin to fall away.

THE EFFECTS OF
CONTRACEPTIVE METHODS

No discussion of contraception would be complete without mention of safe sex as a means to protect oneself from HIV and other sexually transmitted diseases. Although condoms and latex dams are simple enough in concept, some women have difficulty insisting on their use. This is dangerous, as the incidence of AIDS is rising most dramatically among women, particularly heterosexual women.

The need to take precautions changes sexual dynamics, particularly those of foreplay. Ideally, a couple should discuss safe sex in advance, but often the issue rises concurrently with passion. Some women have been pleasantly surprised at how bringing up mutual risks and responsibilities sets them on equal footing with their partners. In heterosexual unions, conventional roles of man as aggressive and woman as passive all but wither away. Foreplay becomes literally playful; acts of securing the condom or placing the dam can be humorously erotic. To compensate for loss of spontaneity, more egalitarian sexual interactions may be experienced.

Although barrier methods are surveyed later in this section, the female condom should be mentioned here. This device consists of a sheath of latex with one open and one closed end, each encircled by a rubber ring. The smaller ring (closed end) is inserted and placed over the cervix; the larger ring remains outside the body, resting over the labia. Originally developed in Europe, this method is only recently available in the United States, so we have little data on user satisfaction. But some women have reported discomfort during intercourse, presumably from the outer ring rubbing against the labia or clitoris—still, the female condom gives a woman the prerogative.

Regarding the more popular methods, we will start with oral contraceptives. Put bluntly, the birth control pill completely wipes out the cyclical pattern of emotional and sexual response we have discussed. The pill works by effecting a state of minipregnancy, with hormone levels high enough to trick the body into believing it's pregnant so that ovulation does not occur. Most formulas combine estrogen and progesterone; others use progesterone only (the minipill). Each of these hormones, should the dose prove excessive, is responsible for specific side effects such as weight gain, acne, breast tenderness, nausea, headaches (other than migraines), and fatigue. (See the chart on page 48.) A woman's response to a particular formula is somewhat unpredictable because much depends on her preexisting balance and sensitivities. This is why a gynecologist may suggest five or six brands before discovering one that is satisfactory.

Ultimately, though, the day-to-day hormone mix is uniform. A woman on birth control pills is hormonally monotone, always the same. Gone are the

...though bleeding when they have taken the last of the batch and hormone levels drop temporarily. This flow is lighter and typically uniform, without variation in length or consistency.

Even sequential pills (triphasic), which attempt to duplicate a more natural rhythm of estrogen and progesterone, produce an artificial pattern ultimately foreign to a woman's own. When clients tell me of their desire to get off the pill, albeit with some reluctance, they often cite the primary reason as wanting to be more in touch with their bodies. As we talk further, what they really seem to miss is being in touch with themselves, their own unique mind-body blend. It's disturbing to think that artificial hormonal influences could alter personality, but considering the singular powers of estrogen and progesterone, such is clearly the case.

At last, women are beginning to find clinical confirmation of their loss of interest in sex when on the pill. Rosemarie Krug, a psychobiologist from the Department of Clinical Neuroendocrinology at the Medical University of Lubeck, ran a study of women's response to erotic imagery, comparing women on the pill to those who were not. Three times a month, study participants were exposed to a series of rapid shots of naked men, babies, women combing their hair, and so on, and were asked to categorize them

ESTROGEN AND PROGESTERONE IMBALANCES

Signs of Estrogen Excess
- nausea and vomiting
- dizziness
- edema
- leg cramps
- increase in breast size
- chloasma (brown pigmentation on face)
- changes in eyesight
- hypertension
- certain headaches (vascular)

Signs of Estrogen Deficiency
- early spotting (days 1 to 14)
- reduced menstrual flow
- nervousness
- painful intercourse due to vaginal changes

Signs of Progesterone Excess
- increased appetite
- tiredness
- depression, mood changes
- breast tenderness
- vaginal yeast infection
- oily skin and scalp
- hirsutism (excess body hair)

Signs of Progesterone Deficiency
- late spotting and breakthrough bleeding (days 15 to 21)
- heavy menstrual flow, with clots
- decreased breast size

Now, let's consider the effects of the intrauterine device on a woman's cycle. With the exception of the Progestasert, the IUD does not directly affect hormonal balance. However, many women do report heavier periods with greater discomfort. Originally, women receiving the IUD were told that these problems were merely mechanical, that the device caused low-grade irritation with side effects of cramping and increased flow. What they were not told was that the IUD does not actually prevent conception, merely implantation of the already fertilized ovum. After all, there is no mechanical barrier to prevent the sperm from meeting the egg. The so-called heavy periods with the IUD are in fact spontaneous miscarriages, month after month after month.

Thus the hormonal effects of the IUD, though indirect, are quite drastic; with conception, dramatic changes in the levels of estrogen and progesterone occur. I recall piecing this realization together many years ago while wearing an IUD. I couldn't wait to get it out! The idea of miscarrying over and over, plus going through intense hormonal changes on a nearly continuous basis, was physically and emotionally offensive to me. I realize that certain women are satisfied with the IUD and consider it a godsend. But so extensively has it been linked to fertility problems (due to uterine scarring, tubal pregnancy and rupture) that it is nearly off the market, except for the Copper 7 and Progestasert devices. The latter works something like the minipill: increased levels of progesterone on a daily basis tend to prevent the egg from maturing and chemically alter the cervical mucus in a way that makes it inhospitable to sperm. Menstrual irregularities are common, such as prolonged bleeding and occasional amenorrhea.

There are two other progesterone-based methods of contraception currently available. Norplant inserts provide up to five years' protection from pregnancy by slowly releasing hormones into a woman's bloodstream. Depo-Provera injections are given every three months. The primary difference between these two methods is the amount of progesterone—Norplant levels are similar to those of the minipill, whereas Depo-Provera is very high-dose. Accordingly, side effects from Depo-Provera are more extreme: cessation of menses, weight gain, breast tenderness and depression that may persist for many months after discontinuation, bone density decrease when used over long periods of time, and dramatic reduction of high-density lipoprotein cholesterol (the good kind, which keeps blood cholesterol levels low). And Norplant not only causes menstrual irregularities similar to the minipill, but may precipitate the development of ovarian cysts.

The nearly foolproof ~~ ~~ ~ ~

~~ ~~~, ~~~~ to produce good results and maintain hormonal balance.[10]

What about the barrier methods? Obviously, these have no physiological effect on a woman's cycle. Local effects and inconveniences are considerable, including chemical irritation from spermicide, lack of spontaneity, messiness, and reduced sensation.

My extensive experience with the cervical cap has led me to favor it both personally and professionally. As compared to the diaphragm, it uses very little spermicide: no additional applications are required for repeated intercourse. It can be left in place for several days and is small enough to be virtually undetectable. A little-known fact about the diaphragm is that although it feels snug when first placed, the vagina expands so much with arousal that even an oversized fit will move and slide around freely during intercourse, readily admitting seminal fluid. Thus the jelly inside the diaphragm becomes so diluted that more must be added before having sex again, hopefully to catch the sperm before they get over the rim. But the cap fits the cervix securely with suction, forming a stable mechanical barrier. In addition, when the user is fertile, the cap retains her mucous secretion so that the natural, sperm-killing acidity of the vagina is maintained (seminal fluid is alkaline, as is fertile mucus; sperm need this in fresh, abundant supply or they die rapidly). Thus the cap works with a woman's chemistry rather than against it, and it is more truly a barrier method than the diaphragm, which relies heavily on chemical effect.

A bonus of cap use is increased familiarity with one's cycle; it is fairly easy to see what phase you are in depending on the type of secretion your cap collects. Also, women who use the cap report less yeast and other vaginal infections than with the diaphragm, since chemical disturbance of vaginal flora is virtually nonexistent.

Having used a diaphragm for 14 years, as well as having fitted them extensively, I know the frustrations of overriding discomfort and disrupted spontaneity. There were numerous occasions I was tempted to leave the diaphragm in the drawer or toss it into the trash can. Eventually, I recognized that much of my resistance was due to reduced levels of sensation during intercourse. Around this time, news of the Graffenburg spot (or G-spot) hit the press, and suddenly it all made sense. By virtue of its design, the front rim of the diaphragm must displace the G-spot in order to lodge behind the pubic bone. No wonder I couldn't feel as much! Once I learned fertility awareness and could safely use my diaphragm only when necessary, I was able to make a real comparison. The problem was solved completely when I switched to the cap; it sits way back on the cervix alone, nowhere near the G-spot.

As mentioned earlier, some women use fertility awareness as birth control, abstaining during the ovulatory phase. However, this may cause considerable frustration, as intense desire must routinely be ignored or expressed in ways other than vaginal/penile intercourse. Increasingly, women in my practice choose to combine fertility awareness with a barrier method of some kind.

A number of women alternate use of the cap or diaphragm with condoms. They say it feels good to share the responsibility, switching back and forth from month to month, or from time to time. A comment from Suzanne: "My partner and I had run the gamut in birth control, and ended up with barrier methods for safety's sake. But it didn't feel right to me to always be the one who had to remember to take charge. It's nice when my partner uses a condom: I can just sit back and relax, and I like the feeling of my body being completely natural. It helps me enjoy sex more."

In the next chapter, we will look at sex and the childbearing cycle, including the fertility dance leading up to conception. Particularly if a woman is aware of her rhythms, she and her partner will be likely to experience conception as it occurs. We will also consider how out-of-sync desires for conception can affect the tone, ease, and frequency of sexual sharing in a relationship.

          Penelope Shuttle and Peter Redgrove, *The Wise Wound* (New York: Richard Marek, 1978).

5.   Taylor, *Red Flower*.

6.   Mary Jane Sherfey, *The Nature and Evolution of Female Sexuality* (New York: Random House, 1973).

7.   Barbara G. Walker, *The Woman's Encyclopedia of Myths and Secrets* (San Francisco: Harper and Row, 1983).

8.   Luisa Francia, *Dragontime*, (Woodstock, NY: Ash Tree Publishing, 1988).

9.   Cutler, *Love Cycles*.

10. Lois Jovanovic and Genell Subak-Sharpe, *Hormones: The Woman's Answer Book*, (New York: Ballantine, 1987).

3

Sexuality, Pr~~~

. your biologically programmed de-
sire for conception from time to time. The urge may
emerge only in midcycle dreams, or you may find yourself fantasiz-
ing about babies and birth with increasing frequency. Sometimes,
when the desire for a baby has built up over a period of time,
women report startling feelings during lovemaking that conception
is somehow imminent, as though birth control can barely hold
back the forces of creation—the dam about to burst. Some women
even report visions of waiting spirits, little boys or girls. As one
said, "We were in the midst of lovemaking that was overwhelming
from the moment it began, so very powerful, when suddenly I got
the image of a little, blond, curly haired boy and I *knew* that I
could conceive that child, that it wanted to come to me. I tried to
tell my partner about it later, but he wasn't ready to hear it—he
thought I was fabricating, I guess. But I never will forget the intensity, the clarity, the ultrareal quality of that moment. From then
on, I knew it was just a matter of time and that we were destined
to have a child together."

No one can really say exactly what brings on such revelations, but they clearly go beyond mere biology. I think couples
deeply in love build up so much intensity in their relationship that
it eventually overflows and demands an outlet, an extension.

Women speak of this fecund state in somewhat mystical terms. Joanne recalls, "I felt like the veil between worlds, this and another place of souls, began to fall away. Soon, all we had to do was touch, and the awareness of that other place, new life just waiting, was all around us."

It follows that couples who have this awareness are likely to be conscious of conception if and when it does occur. Looking back, I can recall the exact moment when each of my children was conceived. Even now, I am surprised by how vivid the memories are, every detail of environment and mood crystal clear, with sensory awareness at its peak. Each time, just moments after orgasm, there was a period of truth and realization, extraordinary and profound, that left me sure and shaking with the knowledge that I had conceived. There was no turning back: I was forever changed!

This picture is somewhat at odds with contemporary notions of conscious conception, which paint it out to be thoroughly planned, predicted, and controlled. More often, at least according to my midwifery clientele, it's less a matter of deliberation than surrender, with conception happening to the couple, rather than the other way around. Commonly, they report, "Well, it wasn't exactly planned; it happened a bit sooner than we expected, but we were open to it and we pretty much knew right away."

For others, things are not so easy and spontaneous. Couples struggling with infertility, who have reduced their lovemaking to a by-the-clock method so that chances of conception are maximized, may be so burdened with anxiety and frustration that immediate awareness of conception is blocked. These same emotions are felt by women who have miscarried and are trying again. Women who have had traumatic abortions may also struggle psychologically, particularly if they have not made their peace with previous losses.

And sometimes, a woman stands alone in her desire to conceive. She and her partner can't come to terms with the issue, or perhaps he is adamantly against becoming a father. There is no easy solution here: as a culture, we have not yet dealt with the unnaturalness of ongoing contraception in intimate relationships. In this regard, women must take the lead and speak of the emotional turmoil and hardship contraceptive compliance can cause. This is not to say that contraception hasn't been a boon for women, enabling them to assume social and political roles of great significance by being free to choose whether and when to have children. But I've heard far too many clients in their late thirties or forties speak wistfully of having children someday when their lives are "together," only to become severely traumatized when they finally realize that it's too late

...when we have material and emotional mastery, or we would be having them in our fifties and sixties. Through parenting we grow and develop, we learn to give unconditionally, to accept small strides day by day, and to make the most of the way things are, rather than wishing them to be different. These are important lessons in human maturation that are otherwise difficult to come by. Nevertheless, when today's woman finds herself desirous of children, she is bombarded with rational considerations and beset with doubts. Her reproductive impulse, at once biological, creative, and evolutionary, tends to be crushed. This, we must work to change. We must reclaim the inherent power of our ability to conceive!

When pregnancy does occur, women undergo a complex series of hormonal, physical, and psychological changes that profoundly affect identity and self-expression. Especially at first, the pregnant state seems utter chaos to many women. But pregnancy can be divided into definite stages and phases that do make sense when viewed as a whole: it is comprised of three trimesters, each lasting approximately 13 weeks and each with its own challenges and characteristics.

THE FIRST TRIMESTER

Even though women seldom show their pregnancies at this stage, major hormonal and physiological changes are taking place. When conception occurs, progesterone and estrogen levels do not dip down as in a typical monthly cycle, but rise even higher, to several times their normal levels. This causes changes throughout the body. The thyroid gland enlarges, which raises the metabolic rate to provide the necessary energy for fetal development and other demands of pregnancy on the mother's body. The adrenal glands produce additional aldosterone to help counter the sodium loss that might otherwise occur with such high levels of estrogen and progesterone. This may account for the fact that many women feel a decreased desire for sex at the beginning of pregnancy, at least in the first weeks.

But this is not the only reason sexual desire may be curtailed. Morning sickness, which occurs with the body's adjustment to elevated hormone levels, is hardly conducive to cuddling and carrying on. In fact, many women feel exceedingly vulnerable in this condition and desire or request new sorts of nurturing behaviors from their partners. The simple act of being brought a bit of dry toast first thing in the morning means more to a woman than comfort alone; it's a measure of her partner's ongoing commitment and concern, and as such, can lead to increased trust and intimacy once nausea is overcome. Other physical changes involve the breasts and particularly the nipples, which become hypersensitive to touch. Alicia reports: "My breasts are rather small and I'm not that confident about them, but when I'm pregnant, they become a focus in our lovemaking." Cheryl sums it up succinctly: "My partner and I have never gotten more pleasure from my breasts than when I was pregnant."

Another inconvenience of early pregnancy is frequent urination, due to uterine enlargement and pressure on the bladder. However, increased circulation in pelvic tissues as a mechanism for uterine growth can also lead to pelvic engorgement, similar to that in premenstrual or ovulatory phases of the monthly cycle. This may cause a woman to wonder what's hit her and whether her desire for deep and forceful penetration is really safe. There has been much debate on this subject over the years; theories regarding deleterious effects of intercourse and orgasm on mother and baby have come and gone. For a while it was thought that orgasm should be strictly avoided, lest subsequent uterine contractions cause oxygen deprivation for the baby. There is no doubt that orgasm causes uterine activity ...

... last trimester, but these findings proved inconclusive due to variables such as stress level, dietary habits, and preexisting health conditions.

On the other hand, if there is a history of miscarriage or episodes of bleeding in the current pregnancy, sexual activity may well be curtailed, at least for the first trimester. It is noteworthy that one in four women have some bleeding in early pregnancy, yet only one in ten miscarry. Particularly if the bleeding coincides with the time of the month menstruation would ordinarily occur, there is less cause for concern. In this case, it seems that the body maintains its old rhythm for a while until new hormonal levels are established, nothing more.

If there is a history of premature labor or birth, sexual activity may be forbidden later in pregnancy, depending on whether the cervix shows any signs of premature softening or opening. Sometimes a woman must stay in bed for some time until her baby is ready to be born, with intercourse and orgasm strictly taboo.

Barring these exceptions, sex brings naturally occurring benefits of increased pelvic circulation, release of tension, and overall muscle toning particularly helpful as preparation for birth. There are immense psychological benefits too, especially in the face of rapid growth and change. Many couples describe their sexual encounters in pregnancy as rebonding experiences, akin in tone to those in the initial phase of their relationship. No wonder, for both are assuming new roles and becoming new people, and are getting to know certain aspects of one another for the first time. And for many there is tremendous freedom in not having to worry about birth control.

A woman's desire in the first trimester may also have something to do with the sex of the child she is carrying. At about six to eight weeks, when the brain is developing, male fetuses are exposed to an enormous dose of testosterone, the level of which is four times that throughout infancy and childhood.[1] Surely, this will have some impact on the mother, quite possibly increasing her libido. By the same token, it may be that a mother's ability to recognize the sex of her unborn has some hormonal basis, since surges of male hormone continue to occur in boys at regular intervals during gestation.

Precisely how the demands of early pregnancy will influence a woman's sexuality depends on her personality, her self-esteem, her desire for the baby, the stability of her primary relationship(s), and various other psychosocial factors. Generally, women in our culture feel somewhat frightened upon confirmation of pregnancy; excited perhaps, but apprehensive nonetheless. This is really a very normal reaction, considering that many of us know little or nothing about childbearing, have never witnessed a birth or even held and comforted a baby. Along with the thrill of being pregnant may come well-founded anxiety about joining the ranks of one of the least acknowledged and most underprivileged groups in our society—mothers! The newly pregnant woman soon learns that society considers motherhood a personal venture that must somehow be done "on the side," squeezed onto an already loaded palette of responsibilities. It is never too early to begin the work of establishing a support system, whether by getting together with other expectant mothers or by forging new alliances with female relatives.

In my book *Energetic Pregnancy*, I explore in some detail women's reactions to specific stages of childbearing according to personality type. A physically oriented woman, for example, may find the natural softening of her body and loss of emotional control due to hormone swings at the onset of pregnancy to be fairly excruciating. She is apt to complain that her body doesn't work anymore; no longer can she make her way by physical force alone. Naturally, this will affect her sexual self-image. The key to her adjustment is to let her feelings flow, while learning more about the unique capabilities of her "   " ' ·

··, ι·-ρ·ισιιαιιγ. Concrete, factual information will offset her tendency to be fanatic.

Then again, the mentally led woman, with a penchant for control and having everything in place, may make her adaptation by the book and yet feel disoriented by surges of emotion and extreme mental states quite beyond her experience. She must find a way to release emotion, connecting mind and body through movement, massage, or anything that facilitates spontaneity and trust in her inner voice. This can add an entirely new dimension to her sexuality. Like the other types, she will face fresh challenges as pregnancy progresses; accordingly, her sexual attitudes and behaviors will continue to come up for scrutiny and transformation.

An oft underrated aspect of pregnancy is the sweeping impact of elevated hormones on a woman's psyche. Or perhaps we hear only the downside, the negative view that paints expectant mothers as borderline crazies, forgetful, hopelessly moody, and foolishly preoccupied. It is, after all, our cultural tendency to consider pregnant women childlike, dressing them in puffed sleeves with little-girl prints. Beyond such minimizing and insulting definitions of their psychological state, we must listen to what pregnant women tell us about themselves. "I've never felt better in my life," is a typical response, or, "I'm finally fulfilled, really myself at last." Consider how well nonpregnant women feel at the monthly estrogen peak—confident, powerful, creative, physically alert, and strong—and juxtapose this with pregnancy when levels are even higher. Elevated progesterone and oxytocin also contribute to a heightened state of awareness, adding an extrasensory dimension.

THE SECOND TRIMESTER

The midpoint of pregnancy is the point of stability. Women love this phase; they feel great and look radiant with pregnant glow. Around 20 weeks, a mother usually feels her baby move for the first time, an event known as quickening—an interesting term, connoting awakening and accelerated awareness. Who quickens, though: baby, mother, or both? In any case, there is no doubt that women at this stage in pregnancy have extraordinary powers of perception, concentration, and recuperation, all of which enhance sexual expression. General equilibrium further contributes to increased libido, as all the basic hormonal and mechanical adjustments of pregnancy have taken place and now begin to blend with the mother's own efforts to eat, exercise, and rest responsively. Beyond simple awareness of fetal movement, some women say they start to get a sense of the baby's personality by how it moves, its rhythms of activity and rest. It follows that a woman might also begin to incorporate her feelings for the baby in lovemaking, as the dyad becomes a triad.

Alice, mother of three, puts it this way:

With each of my pregnancies, I became familiar with my baby a little sooner. The first time, I could barely believe I had a baby in me at all, it was just so overwhelming. Then, I remember an incident with my second. I had the flu and was quite sick, and after a rather violent episode of vomiting I said out loud, "Oh, I hope she's all right," and yes, I had a girl! With the last, though, I felt I knew him right from the start. I would tell people that he was very active, but sweet, and they'd look at me indulgently. It's easy to see now that I was right.

And what about sex with this awareness?

When it comes to sex, I also felt that I had more ability each time to communicate my knowledge of the baby to my partner. Our deep connection

, ...ogen peaks and menses in synchrony—makes possible an even deeper physical empathy in pregnancy that enables both parents to know the baby intimately, even though the nonpregnant partner has no biological link. From Jen, "Sex with Anne when she was pregnant was an ever so much enhanced version of what we had known before. I felt very connected to the baby. Knowing Anne so well, it was easy to differentiate the baby's energy from hers."

Throughout pregnancy, oxytocin levels continue to rise. Oxytocin initiates Braxton-Hicks contractions, which tone the uterus and prepare it for labor. In large amounts, oxytocin has also been shown to cause mood elevation and alleviate depression—perhaps this accounts for feelings of joy and well-being many women experience at this stage of pregnancy. Take ample amounts of oxytocin, mix with high levels of estrogen, progesterone, and vaginal engorgement, and no wonder many women in their second trimester find themselves sexually insatiable, surprising both themselves and their partners. Jeanine states:

To be perfectly honest, I masturbated almost every day. It felt very natural to me. Jack was worried that sex would hurt the baby, but our doctor told him to forget his fears. My vagina was so pliable—he could put two or three fingers inside me and I still wanted more, more pressure. I felt like I was opening up for the baby, but when I had orgasms my muscles squeezed so tight Jack said it practically hurt.

Let's take a closer look at men's reactions to sex in pregnancy. If a man feels concern about jeopardizing the pregnancy during the first trimester, his fear may be further compounded by feeling the baby move in the second. The average male believes a woman's system to be somewhat delicate, and the idea of deep thrusting in the general area that a baby is developing makes certain men squeamish. But there is more. Many men struggle with conflicting images of Madonna/lover, unable to blend the two and hence uncertain of how to relate to a pregnant partner sexually. That a woman nurturing new life might also be blatantly lustful and erotic is the merger of two culturally disparate aspects of femininity into one very powerful whole. (Witness the stir caused by Demi Moore's infamous pose in Vanity Fair: eight months pregnant and wearing nothing more than black bra, panties, and spike heels!) For the outright misogynist, the man deeply at odds with his feminine side, or even the ordinary guy who up to this point has had no idea that such a configuration was possible, there is a strong likelihood of sexual inhibition or shutdown.

What's a woman to do if this occurs? Her midwife or doctor should be able to reassure the expectant father, refer him to a support group or to individual counseling. Nevertheless, deeply ingrained beliefs of this kind are not easy to change, thus the situation may not readily improve. Here is where women must rely on the support of one another, sharing frank discussion with body- and sexuality-affirming activities like dance or exercise. Although it may seem odd at first, singing with others is also good because it frees the heart and opens the throat. There is a recognized neuromuscular association between the mouth and the vagina: if one is tight, so will the other be.

In many cultures, ritual dance of some sort has been regularly practiced by pregnant women. Contrary to popular belief, belly dancing was not developed to please and seduce men, but rather to support and reinforce the efforts of women in labor. The movements of the dance, the rolling of the hips and the undulation of the belly, tend to occur spontaneously during labor in women free of cultural inhibitions. Considering the discomfort and pain of the birth process, a circle of dancing women must have served to remind the mother how to let go, at the same time echoing her emotional and physical respon⸺ ⸺ ⸺

⸺ ⸺ ⸺⸺⸺⸺⸺ can breed distrust and estrangement unless communication lines are kept open. As a midwife, I use the sexual nature of the birth process as a reference point to encourage a woman to stay open as much as possible to her partner. I suggest she experiment with positions, such as being on top or lying on her side, that will give her more control over depth of penetration and rate of thrusting. Labor is, after all, an intensely physical experience; the estimated caloric output of the first birth is equivalent to that of a 50-mile hike! And it also involves the same kind of emotional surrender as spontaneous orgasm.

An important aside here about physical and sexual abuse: more and more women are becoming aware of forgotten or repressed experiences now that support and acceptance are forthcoming. And for many, the emotional vulnerability of pregnancy may trigger recollections for the first time that are doubly difficult to handle if their own parents or other relatives are implicated. Naturally, the accompanying sorrows and fears are apt to interfere with the primary relationship. But, wherever possible, it is better to bring these to the surface while pregnant than to have them arise and interfere with labor, or with mothering itself. Hypnosis can be especially useful for reactivating and healing the past, precisely because pregnancy is such a labile state.

Other psychological barriers to intimacy may involve anxieties about such things as money, role changes, and security. Any woman who finds herself at a sexual impasse while pregnant should make every effort to find assistance.

Here's a relevant account from Mariann:

> I went to a woman's psychotherapy conference while pregnant and took a workshop on sexual abuse. I didn't even know why I was there, really, just for the info, I thought. We went around the room with introductions and after the first few heart-wrenching accounts, I felt somewhat out of place. But after a time, I remembered something that happened to me as a child, something I'd completely blocked out. I guess I thought it was no big deal—I was fondled by a conductor on a train when I was 12—but that day, I relived all of my shame and confusion. I learned that women often tend to minimize these experiences, even though they have considerable impact. Just being aware of what happened to me shed light on certain aspects of my personality and the way I am with sex. Being pregnant, I felt open enough to make some changes.

Again, as regards midpregnancy, no matter what a woman's personal challenges, this is a fine time for integration, a time to find stability and prepare for the changes ahead.

THE THIRD TRIMESTER

By overview, the first trimester is initiation into pregnancy; the second, integration and equilibrium; and the third, completion and transition to labor and birth. Sexuality is often disrupted at this final stage by natural physical discomforts of being so very pregnant and carrying so much extra weight. Sleep may be sporadic as comfortable positions become harder to find, although lying on your side with pillows between your legs and under the belly can help. If there is heartburn, caused by the uterus compressing the stomach and progesterone softening the esophageal valve so that stomach acids rise upward, a woman may find that the only way she can sleep is propped upright. And she may need to urinate several times nightly, due to increased pressure from the baby against the bladder. None of this is particularly conducive to *amour*, but the midday rendezvous or other creative solutions may work. Also, pelvic cartilage is softened considerably by progester-one and estrogen both, so that ordinary pre---

becomes uncomfort---

... this time, as the

, ...xtends the abdominal muscles and pulls ... back out of alignment. Rocking the pelvis while on your hands and knees, standing, or even sitting (while driving, for example) can help tremendously. Of course, pelvic rocking comes naturally during intercourse, as does increased circulation, which can soothe and heal the lower back as well.

Emotionally these are trying times, with mixed feelings over the sexual relationship. Sometimes a woman wants to cling to her partner and hold back time, well aware that the baby will soon be out in the world (or in the middle of the bed) and nothing will ever be quite the same again. Sometimes a woman wants privacy and solitude just to be with the baby, trying to get to know it as well as she can before it is born. Sex may seem extraneous or more for her partner than for herself. Especially when she is thinking of the challenges ahead and her ongoing need for support, a woman may be demanding, moody, fearful. Other times, she will feel fully confident, excited by the future and wanting to make love to her partner with happiness and abandon.

Hormones are at least partially responsible for this range of responses, because they are once again on the move, shifting around erratically in preparation for birth. In the last week or so, a drop in progesterone as a precursor to labor often leads to a loss of water weight, a feeling of lightness, clarity, and well-being. Substances known as prostaglandins, which are fatty acids found in the brain, lungs, kidneys, and prostate gland as well as in seminal and menstrual fluids, also increase at term and may be responsible for labor's onset. Or it may be the fetus that is responsible: it too releases prostaglandins as its brain matures. Whatever the source, prostaglandins are known to soften the cervix and cause uterine contractions. Although oxytocin also serves to stimulate uterine activity, it appears less critical in initiating labor and more important in promoting its progress than prostaglandins.

This is why many doctors and midwives now encourage intercourse at term, especially if the baby is overdue. Seminal fluid is extremely high in prostaglandins and thus may serve to trigger labor. (A substitute may be found in evening primrose oil, a prostaglandin precursor; it is reputed to have a similar effect when rubbed gently on the cervix.) Sheila Kitzinger, author of *Women's Experience of Sex* and numerous books on pregnancy, recommends a particular sexual technique for getting labor going. She advises a woman to make love on her back well supported by pillows under her hips, her partner kneeling between her legs. The woman then places her ankles one at a time on her partner's shoulders. This allows for the deepest possible penetration. After he ejaculates, she is to stay with hips elevated for at least fifteen minutes so that prostaglandins may be well absorbed by the cervix. Then follows nipple stimulation at intervals of ten minutes or so, to stimulate oxytocin's release and subsequent uterine activity. This technique replicates the current medical practice of using prostaglandin suppositories to "ripen" the cervix followed by intravenous pitocin (synthetic oxytocin) drip to induce contractions. Given the choice, most women would probably take the former, both to avoid the intrusion of technology and to enhance intimacy as labor begins.

LABOR AND BIRTH

As labor starts, pregnancy is ending. Many women feel genuine sadness at this, especially if it's to be the last baby or the pregnancy itself has been especially fulfilling. And some may feel trepidation due to the dawning awareness that the only way out of labor is through it. Fortunately, there is a classic burst of energy at labor's onset, due probably to a peak in estrogen ~~ ¹ ¹ influence ~f ~~

...........y physi-
..........u on a woman's genitals! During labor, the entire pelvic area is charged with energy: the vagina, clitoris, rectum, anus, and all supporting tissues and musculature. Women often associate the sensations of labor contractions with those of extremely strong menstrual cramps, but with one important difference. Contractions come in waves, building up steadily instead of taking hold abruptly. Women who have learned to cope with menstrual cramps by relaxing, staying loose, and letting go have a distinct advantage in labor. And here is where the parallels to sexual intercourse begin. Particularly when sex is very passionate and forceful, there may be moments of pain or cramping discomfort with deep thrusting and intense pelvic movement, particularly if the cervix is being hit directly or the uterus is jolted against the intestines. Relaxation, rhythmic breathing, and a change of position can help a woman ease through without losing energy, as she would if she tightened up or shut down emotionally. Especially with orgasm, the ability to surrender and diffuse sensation throughout the body is critical.

Deep relaxation, surrender, letting go: when midwives are asked to disclose the secret of giving birth harmoniously, these are the words we choose. Not merely as metaphor, but as physiological fact, as we will see in the coming section. We will also look closely at how environment affects the spontaneity of the birth process.

FIRST-STAGE LABOR

The first stage is the phase of labor wherein the cervix dilates fully to allow the baby to begin its passage through the vagina, or birth canal, and out into the world. The cervical opening is ordinarily closed or stretchy only a fingertip's worth; now it will dilate to a circle of approximately ten centimeters in diameter. Just how this occurs will be explored in a moment; mostly it's a matter of oxytocin intensifying contractions and bringing them closer together.

But in early labor, up to about four centimeters of dilation, contractions may be scarcely noticeable or may feel more like waves of pelvic warmth "with an edge" than painful cramping. So, how about making love in early labor? Considering the connection between sex and the release of oxytocin, this is really quite a good idea. A caution, though: most practitioners feel that vaginal penetration should be avoided once the waters have broken, lest infection occur. But generally, intercourse in early labor relaxes the pelvis, gets the hormones pumping, and eases both partners into an intimate and relaxed state conducive to ready progress. Especially if labor is slow starting or long and drawn out in the early phase, sex may be just the thing. What's more, couples may find a dimension in lovemaking never before experienced. I have definitely learned my lesson about knocking before entering the labor room, particularly when attending home births. I can think of several times when couples hurriedly pulled clothes back on or grabbed a blanket, only to have me tell them to go right ahead!

Some women feel like staying just shy of orgasm; others do not. Celine reports, "Just being close with our clothes off, being caressed, helped me relax a lot and take the contractions in stride. I don't know why, but kissing was especially good! Even though my partner eventually came inside me, I felt more like taking it easy than building up to orgasm."

Kissing and letting go—remember the neuromuscular association between mouth and vagina? In her wonderful book *Spiritual Midwifery*, Ina May Gaskin tells of one couple she directed to kiss in a certain way: the woman with her lips on top, spread out over her partner's. This led to a tangible shift in labor's intensity and very rapid progress. One of the classic lines from this book is the observation, "The same energy that gets the baby in, gets the baby out."[3]

_ ~~~~. i his is what I call the point of reckoning, of realizing that labor is bigger than you are, beyond your experience or control. Naturally, this is somewhat frightening, especially because it tends to occur fairly early, at just four or five centimeters' dilation. A woman may feel that she has already tried everything and is still not making it. Truth is, she's not going to make it or do it as her ordinary self; she must transform somehow to get through it. As you may surmise, this is also a time when women ask for drugs, particularly if they feel unsupported or exposed.

Imagine yourself struggling with physical sensations much stronger than expected, painful the second you tense up or break your concentration, yet the constant parade of nurses and doctors in and out of your room makes it nearly impossible to let go and relax. You find yourself afraid, wanting to cry out and find relief, move around and change positions, but your circumstances are far too inhibiting. Your attendants are sympathetic and encouraging, but no one is really getting down to your level, looking you in the eye. Though your partner is standing by, he too feels afraid and helpless.

Niles Newton, a remarkable woman who has done much groundbreaking research on birth, breastfeeding, and sexuality, investigated the importance of environmental factors on the birth of mice. She found that births were longer, more difficult, or more obstructed when the mice were placed in unfamiliar surroundings, could not smell or see what they were used to, were moved repeatedly during labor, or were placed in clear (as opposed to opaque) cages. Opposite factors of familiar surroundings, privacy, and stability contributed to spontaneous, easy deliveries.[4]

It was Grantly Dick-Read who first explained how fear or tension can cause pain and lack of progress in labor. The uterus is composed of several muscular layers, the outer with long fibers, the inner with circular fibers. In the absence of fear and tension, oxytocin works on the long fibers, causing them to contract, retract, and become shorter. The inner muscle fibers (which encircle the cervix) stay soft and relaxed, and the shortening of the long fibers gradually pulls the cervix open. But when a woman is tense or frightened, elevated adrenaline levels shunt blood away from the uterus to the extremities and cause the circular fibers of the uterus to become rigid. The two muscle layers then work in opposition so that pain results.[5] Similarly, if you are tense or frightened during intercourse, you are not likely to experience orgasm.

How to avoid all this? Picture yourself in a darkened room with just your partner, the two of you in bed or thereabouts, your midwife or doctor sitting quietly in the corner, coming over now and then to check the baby and offer encouragement but generally unobtrusive, perhaps retiring to an adjacent area so your privacy is complete. You still have to deal with the pain, both the physical intensity and the psychological trauma of "it's not what I expected," but you can speak freely to your partner, you can cry, laugh, shout, whatever suits you as you work together; it is your experience.

A major problem with hospital births is the increasingly routine intervention in otherwise normal labor. Once the decision is made for one intervention, others are likely to follow. For example, when pitocin is used to speed up labor (as per general guidelines that dilation should proceed at a certain rate), contractions may become so unnaturally strong and painful that the mother requires pain relief or becomes less cooperative with the process. These ultrastrong contractions also place stress on the baby by pushing the uterus, which never relaxes completely enough to be well oxygenated. If fetal distress persists, as is likely since by now the mother is sedated and the uterus dependent on artificial stimulation, the probable conclusion is cesarean delivery. Consider that one in five births today is by cesarean section; in some hospitals, as

changes.

Old medical texts teach that less than 5 percent of births involve complications. Our 20 to 30 percent cesarean rate has mostly iatrogenic causes, that is, those generated by technology, procedure, or practitioner. The fact that our malpractice compensation system does not discriminate between acts of fate and genuine negligence has much to do with this—every concrete bit of documentation regarding labor's course and the baby's ongoing condition must be secured in the event of lawsuit. And culturally, we expect a perfect outcome, a perfect baby. Nevertheless, it is a simple fact of life that birth is a mystery that can never be fully circumscribed by a technological approach. Even in the most carefully monitored situations, hemorrhages occur unexpectedly, babies get stuck at the shoulder, cord accidents happen at the last minute, babies and mothers die. The bottom line is that in spite of all our intervention, we have a *higher* perinatal mortality rate than most countries where birth occurs spontaneously and is commonly attended at home.

Whatever your environment, once you make the shift to active labor (contractions long and strong, coming about every five minutes), neurohormones called endorphins will begin to enter your bloodstream. Released during intense physical activity and responsible for the surge of strength, power, and well-being known as the second wind, these are the same substances that cause "runner's high." Once endorphins have kicked in, a woman may actually enjoy labor or may even find it ecstatic. I have told many times the story of one of my clients who was crying and desperate in early labor, only to be smiling and dancing around the room at nine centimeters' dilation. Not every woman can maintain an external focus so far into labor; it depends how strong contractions are and how quickly labor is progressing. Many turn inward, with eyes closed between contractions, apparently dozing or peacefully out of body. Still, there is always the exception, like the woman who laughed, chatted, and ate fried chicken right up to full dilation!

Endorphins are also released during intercourse and lead to the exquisite feeling known as afterglow. But if anesthetics or analgesics are used in labor, stress perception will be minimal and endorphin release may not occur. Although pain may be nearly obliterated by medication, so too will the transcendental feeling many women report in giving birth naturally, particularly at the height of dilation.

What happens next? Even women who have never been pregnant have heard of the transition phase of labor, reputed to be the most difficult of all. Not every woman experiences transition, but for those who do, it occurs somewhere around eight to ten centimeters' dilation. Physically, the cervix continues to dilate even as the baby descends through it and pushes onto the pelvic floor. This leads to mixed, conflicting messages of "relax, stay open, surrender," and "ummh, push, bear down, get busy!" Just when a woman feels she has finally made her peace with letting go, she suddenly becomes compelled to do something, to act. Emotionally, her mood swings wildly; she may swear at her husband or birth attendants. Hormonally, there are ongoing rushes of oxytocin interspersed with surges of adrenaline.

But wait, you say. How can these purportedly conflicting hormones work in concert? According to Michel Odent, there comes a time (generally around the shift from first to second stage) when adrenaline is both physiologic and positive in effect. He

e by identifying two
nhibitory and alpha-
prostaglandin release
of energy just before
rels are thought to be
ng this physiology to
that if threatened in

even have mortal fear
val. She may well cry
n to what is taught in
an should make only
should make the tran-
ble. On the contrary,
es often scream or roar
ng to their feet or into
ame women later revel
," one recalled, "where
of me that had never
—raw, clear, and unbe-
ther, "like some sort of
one of the most sexual
sform a previously shy
ive lover.

ABOR

although second stage
commences with full dilation, some women do not experience the
adrenaline surge and urge to push for some time after, especially if

the baby is still fairly high in the pelvis. Sometimes, if labor has been long or hard thus far, women even sleep or nap as the uterus rests, then wake with clear urges to push. As bearing-down signals get stronger, pressure begins to build in the vagina. What is this sensation like? Imagine an object the size of a grapefruit (the baby's head) pressing on all the sensitive areas deep inside you, combined with a downward squeezing urge something like moving your bowels but multiplied ten times—a whole-body urge, almost like turning inside out, and you have some idea of the sensory magnitude as delivery approaches. No wonder we need a burst of adrenaline to help us through! Physiologically, the uterus has stretched and thinned in the lower segment, while the long fibers have retracted to form a mass at the top, which then pushes the baby downward. And it is primarily the uterus that pushes the baby out, not the mother, although her ability to cooperate with her body makes a difference in ease of progress. Second stage can be 20 minutes of urges so overwhelming that a woman can scarcely catch her breath, or may last several hours with urges of varying length and intensity, sometimes so light she can breathe right through them.

Once again, however, we find medical management at odds with basic physiology; labor and delivery staff seem determined in nearly every case to get the baby out as soon as possible. Women are told to draw their legs back forcibly, hold a breath as long as possible, and push their guts out with every contraction. This is rather like trying to force orgasm, riding over the rhythm instead of with it. To put it another way: under which circumstances might you find it easier to have an orgasm: with someone barking orders at you every step of the way, or when free to surrender your body and let it take you? Most probably, aggressive management of second stage is a remnant of the old notion that it is dangerous for both mother and baby to let the fetal head "pound the perineum". If anything, forced and insensitive pushing is apt to cause damage to vaginal tissues, at the same time depriving the baby of oxygen. As demonstrated by Roberto Caldeyro-Barcia, unnaturally long periods of maternal breath-holding can lead to fetal acidosis and distress.[7] Sheila Kitzinger goes so far as to say that the problem is that of imposing a male-ejaculation model on the pushing process, for which the variable-intensity, multiple-orgasm female model is imminently more suitable.

When a woman in second stage is unfettered by outside direction she will, in fact, breathe very much as she would during sexual excitation and orgasm: up to three times more rapidly than usual, with periods of breath-holding punctuated by gasps, groans, or cries. Women allowed ... ...

... ... her own baby, sensing exactly when she can take more stretch and when to ease up, effortlessly breathing her baby out. After a huge episiotomy (a cut to enlarge the birth canal) with my first child, I was determined not to tear with my second, so I really tuned in during pushing, just closed my eyes and did it all from the inside. I could feel *everything,* the precise contours of my daughter's head as I eased it out, even her little shoulders and body as she whooshed and squiggled through. It was absolutely the most exquisite thing I have ever felt in my life. Later, my midwives said they wished they had the birth on tape, it was so perfectly controlled. But "controlled" is not the way I would describe my process, as I wasn't really holding back. Beyond attunement, there was union, perfect union.

There has been some interesting research regarding vaginal stimulation in labor and subsequent bonding behaviors. Vaginal stimulation has been shown to be an important determinant of bonding in sheep.[8] When vaginal stimulation by vibrator was given to nonpregnant ewes primed with estrogen and progesterone, they responded to newborn lambs with a full range of bonding behavior. With similar stimulation, recently delivered ewes already bonded to their own lambs stopped rejective behavior to alien lambs and accepted them as their own. Further, Krehbiel and co-

workers (1982)[9] found that by giving peridural (pelvic floor) anesthetics to ewes during labor, particularly if given early, maternal
behavior was severely altered; seven of the eight first-time mothers
failed to show any normal bonding behavior during the first half
hour. Animals that had given birth before responded less noticeably, but still showed some effects. Perhaps the choice of epidural
anesthesia (which numbs to a greater extent than does peridural)
is not so benign as we have thought. I have noticed that once an
epidural is administered, a woman becomes more a spectator than
a participant, although epidurals in low doses to aid in the event of
obstruction can sometimes make the difference between vaginal
birth and cesarean section.

All of this raises yet another issue, that of vaginal tearing
with delivery. Isn't it better to have an episiotomy, rather than
being stretched out or torn? And if an episiotomy is going to be
necessary, then mustn't the area be numbed in advance anyway?

Here we have one of the biggest lies perpetuated by modern
obstetrics: that the human vagina is somehow inadequate to the
task of delivery and must be surgically enhanced. Most women
don't realize that the surface of the vagina is covered with ruggae,
accordion-like folds of tissue that expand naturally under the hormonal influence of parturition (giving birth). When a woman is
relaxed and centered during the delivery, not rushed but well supported, she will generally give birth without a nick or with abra-
sions so minor they require no treatment. And despite beliefs to
the contrary, nice, clean episiotomy cuts are not easier to heal
than tears that do require stitches: the irregular edges of a tear
actually mesh together better and close more quickly. Finally, it is
much easier to regain sexual pleasure and muscle response after
repair of a tear than an episiotomy. Tears frequently skim the surface, but in doing an episiotomy one is obliged to cut through
muscle. The result is a wall of scar tissue, both inflexible and
numb to sensation.

But what about overall snugness, you may wonder? How can
an area that has been stretched so completely ever regain its former tone? And isn't that what the "husband's stitch" is for? Theo-

retically, yes—but that final excessively tight stitch is external, right at the base of the vaginal opening, and does little more than cause pain and distress with intercourse. Pleasurable friction comes not at the opening but from muscles immediately inside the vagina, which extend upward several inches or so. Although it is possible to create a tight vaginal opening with surgical repair, scarred areas inside will be rigid, surrounding muscles flaccid, and the entire area d....f.... .. . . .

...pleasurable a partner than one with deep-tissue trauma and repair (at least until the healing occurs, which can take many months).

In the 1950s, when the "husband's knot" became a standard part of repair technique, women were not taught pelvic floor exercises (detailed in Chapter 4), and few explored their own musculature for fear of hurting themselves or doing something "dirty." Sexual mores were based on male gratification; little was known or understood about female sexual response. Times have changed; women are more in possession of their own bodies and most have no qualms about putting fingers into the vagina to aid them in toning the muscles there. In fact, women who are in touch with themselves this way and who have been prepared to give birth without an episiotomy but, at the last minute, are given one anyway, often feel violated and emotionally traumatized. As one woman, Jan, recalled of her first birth, "I felt I was doing a good job, easing my baby out nicely, when suddenly and for no apparent reason my doctor changed his mind and cut me. I felt like, 'Oh . . . well, okay, I give up . . . guess I'm not good enough.' I lost all feeling, and he took control." In over 300 deliveries, I have had to perform an episiotomy only five times, due to last-minute fetal distress necessitating immediate delivery. And I have had very few women tear. My secrets: engage the woman in sensitive breathing, use hot compresses and perineal massage, and help her to take it slowly.

DELIVERY

At the final moment of crowning, when the widest part of the head stretches the vaginal opening to its maximum, some women love either to look in a mirror or to reach down and feel, for the first time, their little one. Sometimes this brings an overwhelming flood of emotion, and the baby is born in an orgasm of delivery. Women describe the moment of delivery as the high point of their lives, a pinnacle emotionally and physically. All the waiting and wondering, all the hopes and fears are finally unleashed and allowed to rush forward as the baby swooshes out and utters its first cry.

If she feels like it, the mother can reach down and lift the baby up when it is still partly inside her: something she will never forget. The baby is wet, warm, incredibly fragile yet surprisingly strong. It smells sweetly of birth. She touches its little hands and feet and then finds herself falling into its eyes, seeing the faces of relatives and ancestors, feeling past and future unite simultaneously. Birth is a stunning and overwhelming victory for a woman, especially when she has retained her power and knows she has given it her all.

In the next chapter, we will explore the tender and tempestuous postpartum period, and look at how sexual identity and self-expression are affected and transformed by the presence of a newborn.

1. Elizabeth Davis, *Energetic Pregnancy* (Berkeley, Calif.: Celestial Arts, 1988).

2. Niles Newton and Charlotte Modahl, "New Frontiers of Oxytocin Research," *Free Woman: Women's Health in the 1990s* (Canforth: Pantheon Publishing Group, 1989).

3. Ina May Gaskin, *Spiritual Midwifery* third edition (Summertown, TN: Book Publishing Co., 1990).

4. Niles Newton, Michael Newton and Donald Foshee, "Experimental Inhibition of Labor Through Environmental Disturbance," *Obstetrics and Gynecology*, vol. 27 (1966).

5. Grantly Dick-Read, *Childbirth Without Fear* (New York: Harper and Row, 1959).

—indsay, vaginal Stimulation: An Important Determinant of Maternal Bonding in Sheep," *Science*, vol. 219 (1983).

9. D. Krehbiel, P. Poindron, F. Levy, and M.J. Podhomme, "Peridural Anesthesia Disturbs Maternal Behavior in Primiparous and Multiparous Parturient Ewes," *Physiology and Behavior*, vol. 40 (1982).

4

...ory one of the most tempestuous and challenging phases of a woman's life. It's been said that the relative pleasure and exhilaration of pregnancy and birth are but preparation for the grueling adjustments postpartum. I often tell women that the first six weeks of caring for a newborn baby is the hardest work they will ever do. The changes that must be made in adding another member to the family group and in altering the household routine are far from minor. The stress of it all may well lead a woman to wonder whether there is sex after birth.

THE RECOVERY PROCESS

With a little patience and creativity, sex usually comes back better than ever, even though modifications will be called for. But to truly understand sexuality during this phase, we must first look at the physical process of recovery as well as that of lactation.

In the first few moments following delivery, fresh spurts of oxytocin are released to contract the uterus and shear off the placenta. As the baby is put to the breast, nipple stimulation triggers additional oxytocin, which shrinks the uterus down to the size of a grapefruit. Over the next ten days or so, continued release of oxytocin will contract the uterus back to its pre-pregnant size. When a woman breastfeeds, oxytocin levels rise even higher according to frequency of nursing, which in the first few weeks may occur as often as every hour or two. The extra boost serves to contract and tone the upper vaginal area (or vault), a process that takes place much more slowly in women who bottlefeed.

Breastfeeding is initiated in part by the hormone prolactin, which is released as estrogen and progesterone levels drop with delivery. Ongoing milk production is due to sucking stimulation of the breasts; the more the baby sucks, the more milk the mother will produce, provided she has adequate rest, food, and drink. Let-down of milk is caused by oxytocin's release, most directly by nipple stimulation.

What does let-down feel like? Generally, it's very pleasurable. There is a tingling in the breasts, a tightening as they fill, and a longing for release. We have, I think, a ready correlation to what men experience with arousal. There is definitely an urgency to find a partner: a mother experiencing let-down really *wants* her baby. No wonder women find breastfeeding to be a sexual experience! Sometimes, the accompanying uterine and vaginal contractions even lead to orgasm. At the very least, unless a woman has over-riding inhibitions, breastfeeding is physically satisfying and fulfilling. There is a characteristic feeling of warmth and well-being that encompasses body and soul: a flow of energy that is soothing and healing. And it is a shared experience. The baby responds with love and desire; its little hands stroke the breast, its body presses forward (as it gets older), and its toes may curl rhythmically. Just as sexual intercourse bonds emotionally healthy adults together, so does breastfeeding bond mother and child. We are little accustomed to thinking of babies (or children) as having sexual needs, but to a certain extent, they do. Close to our most basic definition of sexual desire is the physical and emotional urge for intimacy that is with us from birth.

Niles Newton and Charlotte Modahl found that mood changes caused by breastfeeding are very much like those that occur with intercourse and orgasm. On the other hand, women who bottle-feed their babies have been shown to have higher levels of depression, anxiety, stress, regression, and guilt on a day-to-day basis than mothers who breastfeed.[1] According to the research of E. B. Thoman and coworkers, lactating women have shown a suppression of adrenaline release and accompanying neurological activity in response to various kinds of trauma.[2] It would seem that the release of oxytocin through breastfeeding is something of a biological perk to help women buffer stress and make it through the physical challenges of this ~h~

...cks postpartum, all these
...ttt back to normal. This is not a smooth, even process of change but an erratic and fitful one. Hormones ebb, flow, and intricately readjust. The resulting hot flushes and cold spells, night sweats, and mood swings lead this to be a biologically and emotionally charged period for women and their families.

EMOTIONAL CHANGE AND ADJUSTMENT

Distinguishing the biologically induced mood swings of this period from those based on more far-reaching socioemotional concerns is a real challenge, especially for a woman going it alone. That we treat the new mother as though nothing has changed, and expect that she will be back on her feet and in charge of her affairs in a matter of days, is the height of denial, considering the monumental task of adjusting to a new way of life. And what is she to think, alone at home in the midst of total turmoil, except that she is weak, incompetent, or totally out of her mind? In many cultures, some observation is made of the lying-in period, a time when women are expected to rest and recover. Sometimes this lasts six weeks, sometimes only ten days, but in any case there is acknowledgment of the mother's need to be cared for completely as she learns to take care of her baby. A well-supported mother will bond better, love more deeply, and be better able to distinguish the needs of her child from her own. Good care frees her to develop as an individual; it gives her a healthy foundation on which to base her social interactions and contributions. Her child reaps the benefits of security and respect for its own process of growth. Yes, care of new mothers assures survival of the species, but more than that, it positively affects a culture's quality of life.

Postpartum customs in Native American and Indonesian cultures often involve the use of heat, either heating the room or building a fire near or under the mother's bed so she may be unclothed, nurse spontaneously, feel relaxed and at ease. Far from the overwhelming isolation a new mother experiences in the so-called developed world, here she is surrounded by her peers and extended family, women who are knowledgeable and loving. They feed her, laugh with her, counsel her, marvel at the miracle of her newborn child, and feel enriched by contact with her. In the Philippines, the new mother is considered to be in such a state of vulnerability and grace that should she die in the first 40 days postpartum, her soul will automatically go to heaven.

When a woman is not well cared for at this time, there are complex, often long-term effects on her body, personality, and sexuality. Even though we have noted oxytocin's ability to buffer stress, there are definitely limits. If a woman is forced out of bed or back to work too soon, overproduction of adrenaline will severely inhibit recovery. As Newton states, "Oxytocin reflexes can be severely inhibited by environmental disturbances, emotional upset or pain."[3] What this really means is that the Amazon concept of postpartum recovery is mostly myth: women are *not* intended to give birth in the bushes and jump back on their horses. The notoriously high incidence of postpartum depression in the United States has frustrated biological needs at its root. Without adequate rest, recuperation is grueling and prolonged, and sex is the last thing on a woman's mind.

But there are other factors, too. The same cultural ideology that deems it appropriate to abandon the new mother further chal-

lenges her identity. As she assumes her new role, she may experience painful losses. Single friends may abandon her, finding it
impossible to relate to what she and her family are experiencing.
Her primary relationship is altered and may become somewhat
strained. She herself is inextricably changed; her old routines and
ways of handling daily business are in total upheaval. Privacy
seems a thing of the past, at least at the beginning.

On a practical l. . l. . . .

. . . . .g . . . . guided advice sinks deep; criti-
cism is not easily forgotten.

More than anything else, giving birth brings home the fact
that control of life is just an illusion. Hopefully, a woman has a
positive and exhilarating experience in making this discovery; if
not, her self-esteem may be seriously damaged. This too can lead
to lingering depression, particularly when combined with other
postpartum stresses. One of my primary tasks as a midwife is to do
postpartum home visits to see how my clients are healing and
adjusting. Women often raise questions and express anxiety about
their "performance" or behavior in giving birth as early as day
three, and sometimes call in tearful panic during the weeks that
follow for more discussion, more reassurance. This is particularly
true if the birth has been difficult or the outcome somehow disappointing. Certainly the course of acceptance will be rocky if there
are problems with the baby's health or physical condition. But a
woman can have a perfectly beautiful and healthy baby and still be
devastated by how birth went for her. Until very recently, women
were denied the right to grieve over their own experience; as my
mother was told when she complained to her doctor about the
indignities she suffered at the hands of hospital staff, "If the cake
is good, eat it!" She told me this just days after my own traumatic

first delivery, and it remains one of the pivotal moments in my life when I said to myself, "No, this is not enough, I am worth more than that, *women* are worth more than that!"

Yet another aspect in a woman's recovery has to do with how well she has bonded to her baby. Much research has been done in this area, most of it showing damaging effects if mother and baby are separated for more than a few minutes during the first few hours, especially immediately after birth. Animals thus separated respond in classic ways: the newborn creature will bond with whatever is available (even another species, or something mechanical), and the mother will reject her young if later reintroduced. This is powerful genetic programming meant to ensure survival, and when it is disrupted in the human sphere a woman feels herself rather like Humpty Dumpty: who can put the pieces back together again? Beyond immediate bonding, if a woman stays in the hospital for any time at all, nurses may feel obliged or may choose to begin caring for the baby: dressing it, changing its diaper, comforting it. But all of these are critical tasks that the mother needs to experience herself in order to develop maternal instinct and her own foundation for caregiving.

It is both curious and disappointing that in her recent book, *Revolution from Within*, Gloria Steinem traces damage to self-esteem only so far back as the early years. She acknowledges that, "As infants and small children, we cannot possibly earn our welcome in this world,"[4] but fails to link this to experience at birth. She also stresses the importance of "honoring the wisdom of the body," yet seems unaware of how deeply this wisdom can be violated by birth trauma and how devastating the effect on self-esteem. Indeed, if birth has been emotionally traumatic and bonding was disrupted, a chain reaction of missed communication and ineffective behavior between mother and baby may make efforts to improve the relationship later on frustrating and exceedingly difficult.

And now it is time to tie all this to postpartum sexuality. At the most basic level, the key to sexual health and happiness in this phase has to do with the mother recognizing her new self, working out her birth experience, accepting her changed role, and then deepening her attachment to her baby. If she is able to do all this, she will generally return to her partner with great enthusiasm. There are certain practical considerations regarding sex at this time, but ultimately, sex postpartum is not about timing and technique any more than it is at any other phase of a woman's life. The reason that many guidebooks take this focus is that identifying and dealing with the ...ded...

...... a ....g.... level of sexual interest than bottle-feeding mothers. They were also, as a group, more interested in as rapid a return as possible to sexual activity with their partners.[5]

Breastfeeding provides, for many women, an important way to reestablish bonds that have been broken by difficult birth. Counseling is increasingly available for women who want help in this area. And in spite of the crucial importance of bonding at birth, we human females are distinct from other mammals in that we have the intelligence and reason to deliberately re-create our bonds with our young. This is far from easy but it definitely can be done.

PRACTICALITIES OF POSTPARTUM SEX

Now we are ready to discuss the brass tacks of postpartum sexuality. Especially at first, women are greatly concerned about their internal healing and potential vulnerability during intercourse, particularly if they have had stitches.

Fear is often triggered by either pain or stiffness at the site of injury. Most doctors have women return for a checkup around six weeks postpartum to determine degree of recovery, readiness for intercourse, and appropriate contraception. But many women are told little or nothing of how to care for the perineum in the interim, nor such things to watch for as swelling, inflammation, and signs of infection. Pain as a signal for attention may go unnoticed if a woman is taking painkillers during the first few days (the most critical time for healing).

I suggest that women use ice packs for the first day or so to reduce swelling, then switch to sitz baths several times a day using hot water with selected herbs. Nothing speeds healing faster than heat, and soaking is far superior to topical application when it comes to stimulating circulation. Fresh ginger can be added to the soaking solution to relieve the itching that often occurs as stitches dissolve and skin heals. Grate the root (a three- or four-inch root will do fine) into a large pot of water, simmer 20 minutes, strain, and divide into two portions. Save one for later in the day, and dilute the first with water in the sitz bath unit (a special plastic tub that fits directly over the toilet seat, readily available at most hardware stores). After soaking for 20 minutes or so, thoroughly dry the perineum and leave exposed to air or sunlight another 10 minutes before putting on a fresh pad (use a hair dryer to speed the process). If the area feels at all sticky, aloe vera gel will dry and soothe the tissues. Avoid vitamin E or other oil-based ointments until the skin is healed over, as these tend to keep edges from closing.

Despite the six-week ban on sex, some women go ahead and have it anyway before returning to their practitioner for the official okay. Sometimes this is fine; then again, the experience may be so fraught with anxiety and not a little pain that it is both worrisome and disappointing. Why the time limit at all? Ordinarily, it takes about ten days for the uterus to return to normal size and the cervix to close securely. Sex during this time is correlated to bleeding beyond the normal postpartum flow. There may also be some risk of uterine infection, although this has never been well documented. Stitches are a major contraindication; they take a week or so to dissolve and at least two more to heal. A woman who has had a repair should really have herself checked before intercourse, even if it means scheduling an appointment earlier than her practitioner expects or recommends.

Other women are so anxious about "the first time" that even the official all-clear is not enough. In this case, preliminary self-massage can help, particularly in areas with scar tissue. The wall-like ridge characteristic of episiotomy can be softened and relaxed by thumb or finger pressure, using a little oil (make sure to wash your hands before h... "· · ·

.... will increase spontaneously if a mother stops nursing, or may resume gradually as she introduces solid foods and the baby nurses less often. There are exceptions, though. Some women nurse their babies (or even toddlers) just once or twice a day and still do not resume their normal cycles. Others may nurse exclusively and have milk in abundance, yet start menstruating as early as six weeks postpartum. The reasons for this discrepancy are uncertain. A number of my clients have observed that early sexual activity (within the first two weeks postpartum) seemed to cause them to start menstruating within the following month or two. No harm in this; certainly, a woman's sex life will benefit. But babies tend to be fussier when their mothers are menstruating, and women may experience a struggle of their own with PMS, brought on by sleep deprivation and general fatigue. Although coping on these days is something of a strain, estrogen's return serves to compensate.

If adequately repaired and cared for, the perineum should be fully healed after six weeks no matter how extensive the damage. I recently saw a woman who had been suffering for seven months with pain and bleeding during intercourse. She had been back to see her doctor, who offered little advice or assistance. Unfortunately, he was also a relative, so she hesitated to seek a second

NEW MOTHER

A week after our child was born,
you cornered me in the spare room
and we sank down on the bed.
You kissed me and kissed me, my milk undid its
burning slip-knot through my nipples,
soaking my shirt. All week I had smelled of milk,
fresh milk, sour. I began to throb:
my sex had been torn easily as cloth by the
crown of her head, I'd been cut with a knife and
sewn, the stitches pulling at my skin—
and the first time you're broken, you don't know
you'll be healed again, better than before.
I lay in fear and blood and milk
while you kissed and kissed me, your lips hot and swollen
as a teen-age boy's, your sex dry and big,
all of you so tender, you hung over me,
over the nest of the stitches, over the
splitting and tearing, with the patience of someone who
finds a wounded animal in the woods
and stays with it, not leaving its side
until it is whole, until it can run again.

From *The Dead and the Living* by Sharon Olds (New York: Alfred Knopf,
1984).

opinion lest word get back to him. As I suspected, she had been sewn up too tightly (the so-called "husband's stitch"). Even with gentle pressure to the area, drops of blood appeared as the skin tore ever so slightly apart. She and her partner were quite frustrated and miserable. Ultimately, she had to have reconstructive surgery.

Bleeding without pain is normal for up to six weeks but should be fairly light f...

...have about resuming sex is whether or not they will still be satisfactory in bed, whether there will be adequate tone in the vaginal muscles to bring the accustomed pleasure. Usually, some tone is lost at delivery, although breastfeeding naturally helps to restore it. And pelvic floor exercises can be started as early as day one. These aren't particularly easy at first (it is hard enough just to remember to do them), but often they feel more natural and effective if done while breastfeeding. There are two basic movements: one, a longitudinal stroking motion within the vagina as if one were caressing a soft fruit and squeezing out the juice; the other, a quick, snapping movement lower down, near the vaginal opening. These should feel challenging but stimulating and pleasurable. And there is nothing wrong with putting fingers inside to check effectiveness and progress. The use of these movements is actually part of both Tantric and Kundalini traditions whereby women trigger the flow of energy up the spine and throughout the body to enliven awareness and promote well-being. These movements also occur naturally with orgasm, thus sex itself is a great way to re-tone the vagina.

Here are several accounts of first sex postpartum that serve to illustrate both the awkwardness and transformation possible at this time. First from Tessa:

We had been through so much with the birth, John and I, which we planned for home but ended up having in the hospital. There were complications, for me and the baby, but I managed to [give] birth without needing a Cesarean. Then we had to stay in the hospital because of concerns for our son, and my husband was totally drawn into caring for us both. He was down in the nursery when they needed to do tests, talking to the staff, protecting the baby and bringing him right back to me. When we got home we were utterly exhausted, but that very night we made love. I knew I shouldn't (it was only the third day), but we couldn't help it, we had to unite, the urge was irresistible. It was, I think, the most intimate, powerful, and explosive sex we've ever had. It just burst from both of us—we had been so close in pregnancy, and we really reached deep for each other, to get back to ourselves and heal what happened with the birth. I had a little bleeding after, but it was worth it. I'll never forget it.

And from Christine:

I waited a full four weeks, but Jarred was at his limit. I hadn't been to the doctor yet, but I'd been looking in a mirror and feeling around, and everything seemed fine. Well, when he entered me it felt so different that I think it shocked us both. The part that had stitches felt numb and stiff, and the rest of me felt all loose and out of control. But Jarred kept saying I felt so good, so warm, so soft that I put my fears aside and let myself go. Then I came, milk started spurting from my breasts, and the baby started crying like it somehow got the signal. I went to get the baby and brought it into bed to nurse while Jarred licked milk from the other nipple—not exactly what I'd expected, but pretty satisfying all in all.

Leaking milk, by the way, is normal with orgasm since the natural release of oxytocin triggers let-down. It has also been noted that the hormone prolactin tends to synchronize mother/infant sleeping cycles, causing a sort of physiological empathy between the two.

This brings us to yet another area of concern, that of sleeping arrangements for the baby. In the last few decades, family sleeping (baby or children in bed with the parents) has seen a surge of popularity. Reports from those who have tried this are somewhat mixed but basically positive. At least in the beginning having the baby in the

pediatrician colleague suggests putting the baby in its own bassinet next to the parents for at least part of the night, right from the beginning. This may help the baby get used to sleeping alone, at least parttime. One mother told me that when she and her husband decided to move the crib into a separate room, their daughter suddenly began sleeping through the night. (Apparently she had been disturbed by her parents' noises.) Not that sleeping all night in solitude is common for most little ones; children as old as five or six may still get into their parents' bed in the wee hours of the morning.

So how does this work in terms of sex? It depends on the age of the child; if yours is still an infant and you find yourself interrupted in the middle of something sweet, you can probably continue and get away with it. Many women report the stop-gap solution of nursing the baby while making love: an odd juggle of maternal and passionate emotions, but ultimately practical.

The infant turned toddler will probably be too aware for this sort of thing. Still, be sure to let your little one see you and your partner cozily together, hugging and kissing, lest this behavior lead to anxiety should she or he come upon you unawares. Of course, any child will be less jealous and possessive if regularly given lots of love and affection.

Ultimately, new parents make do. And they become creative, seeking out other times and places for intimate rendezvous. See the forthcoming section, "Recapturing Intimacy," for further suggestions.

SEXUAL INHIBITION AND DYSFUNCTION

Sometimes, sexuality is affected by more than practical concerns or typical adjustments. We have discussed already how sleep deprivation and lack of support can lead to transitory depression; if there are serious setbacks in recuperation or traumatic events such as death in the family, loss of a job, or an unexpected move, loss of libido can easily occur.

And there may be deep-seated ambivalence about sexual roles and identity on the father's part. For a man who has been secretly harboring the double-standard view of women (Madonna/whore), now may come a time when this can no longer be concealed. A man well able to love his partner passionately through pregnancy and birth may feel deeply uncomfortable relating to her as a mother. She may notice that he seems hesitant to touch her and think it's because she has lost her looks, is too stretched out inside, or is no longer sexually enticing. But the real reason is usually the aforementioned programming that many men are challenged to handle at this point. Some do so by having affairs, sad to say, while others plunge into their work or other outside efforts. Either way, it's no good for the marriage, and some sort of intervention is called for. Bear in mind that the postpartum period may be one of the first and most critical turning points for a man in reviewing misogynist thinking. There is nothing easy about this process, but it can lead in the long run to genuine coparenting and more egalitarian and intimate ways of living and loving.

For her own part, a woman may feel inhibited from time to time as she struggles with conflicts over her roles of mother, lover, and career woman. As long as she reassures her partner that these are her concerns and have nothing to do with his or her adequacy,

they will be much better off. It's all a matter of setting boundaries—something of a taboo for women in this culture. But personal
boundaries are crucial to one's sanity, self-esteem, and development. Under changed circumstances, as in the postpartum period,
new boundaries must be established. New mothers have tremendous need to conserve energy, muster strength repeatedly, and say no
to anything that conflicts with their instincts. Setting boundaries
means being straight...

...both parents feel they must work? Let's
face it—this is not one of those honeymoon times in a couple's life
when sex is a breeze. This needn't cause panic if you take a broad
view. That is what marriage and partnership is all about: the long-
term view. It is great to be able to get it together enough to
initiate new life, but that is just the beginning. When we start
having sex to learn and grow, when we can engage without expectation and with the maturity to take from sex whatever we find,
we have entered another stage of sexual development. Postpartum
naturally initiates this evolution.

RECAPTURING INTIMACY

Ideally, intimacy is not interrupted or in any way lost in the process of giving birth. But there is change, as we have discussed, and
sometimes a couple must work to reestablish closeness and trust.
This means talking about sex, communicating hurt, fears, and desires more openly than ever. With a baby around, it also means
making the effort to be emotionally and sexually available to one
another, even when not fully in the mood. It means picking up
wherever the two of you left off, even though days may intervene,
keeping closeness in heart and deed.

Sylvia reports:

I felt very estranged from my body and so tired all the time I didn't want sex at all. Mark, on the other hand, would put pressure on me. Then I'd get in the mood, and he'd be too tired or something. Finally, I got in the habit of shutting him out, until one day he actually broke down and told me how much he missed me, missed our closeness. Really, I had forgotten that he cared, that I cared. The birth just turned me upside down, I guess, and I was so involved with the baby.

I told him what it was like for me, how exhausted and used up I felt, and as we talked, one thing led to another and we were making love. It sure wasn't perfect (the baby actually interrupted with a nursing) but it was *real.* You know that quality, when sex is ultrareal? It was raw, it was different, it was new—we were three now, instead of two, more instead of less. Once I saw this, staying connected to Mark became easier. We got really good at blending sex into ordinary, day-to-day things we did, so that when we were alone, we got intimate quite quickly. I felt like I had discovered some secret to happy marriage and wondered, "How come no one ever told me about this?"

Here are a few well-seasoned tips for keeping the fires burning:

✦ **Have some ritual in your sex life.** Choose a night once a week to have dinner, wine, and a video after the baby is asleep, then have sex right there on the floor, on the couch, in the spare bed, or wherever takes your fancy. Even if you are interrupted and can't resume, you know another special evening is only a week away.

✦ **Get out.** Find a good babysitter willing to commit herself to a certain night each week. Choose someone you know and trust or seek recommendations from friends. It makes a difference to go out on a regular basis: the benefits build up. Once out, you will tend to talk mostly about the baby, but try to talk about yourselves, too.

✦ **Make cooking and housework as easy as possible.** If you ever planned to treat yourself to hired help, now is definitely the time. Buy a slow cooker, Dutch oven, or microwave for meals that practically cook themselves. Many birth practitioners recommend that a pregnant woman

your kids, yourself. Call good friends for a chat and some silliness. Let your heart be light, and look on the bright side of difficult situations.

✦ **Try not to burden your partner with grim realities,** at least not on the emotional level. If you can translate these into specific needs, okay, but otherwise forget it. Take responsibility for your feelings. Find other women to talk to for solace and inspiration.

✦ **Know that this wild and crazy time will pass.** Keep the long-term view in mind, plan your first weekend (or week long) getaway with pleasure, and keep the faith.

Finally, it's important to note that against all the odds, a fair number of women feel their sexual understanding and power greatly enhanced by giving birth. Some have orgasms for the first time in their lives. This is probably because birth partners a woman primarily with herself; the particulars of letting go and surrendering come ultimately from within her. Especially if she has been buffeted around by male needs, desires, and opinions about sex, this can come as quite a revelation.

As Cassie says: "I never had orgasms like I did after giving birth. When I was pushing my daughter out, I got more than connected to my vaginal muscles: I *became* them. My strength was incredible, my timing exquisite. Before, when I made love it was me up here, vagina down there. But now my consciousness and intelligence are fully inside me. I'm not afraid to do or try anything with my body; its power belongs to me. Once you've let go giving birth, letting go with sex can take you to places you've never dreamed of."

1. Niles Newton and Charlotte Modahl, "Mood State Differences Between Breast and Bottle-Feeding Mothers," *Newton on Breastfeeding* (Seattle: Birth and Life Bookstore, 1990).

2. E.B. Thoman, A. Wetzel, and S. Levine, "Lactation Prevents Disruption of Temperature Regulation and Suppresses Adrenocortical Activity in Rats," *Communicative Behavior in Biology*, vol. 2, part A (1968).

3. Niles Newton, "The Role of the Oxytocin Reflexes in Three Interpersonal Reproductive Acts: Coitus, Birth and Breastfeeding," *Newton on Breastfeeding* (Seattle: Birth and Life Bookstore, 1990).

4. Gloria Steinem, *Revolution From Within* (Boston: Little, Brown, 1992).

5. W.H. Masters and V.E. Johnson, *Human Sexual Response* (Boston: Little, Brown, 1966).

5

gle, often frantically, the demands of work, family, and personal relationships. Particularly if partnered with men, we continue to do the majority of the housework; we run errands, pay the bills, buy the clothing, supervise household repairs, cook, and do laundry. We often serve as primary go-between with our children's teachers; we make time for parents' evenings and help with homework on a regular basis. If we are lucky, once in a while we lunch with a friend—that is, if we can find time, what with obligatory entertaining and our kids' extracurricular schedules. If we happen also to be self-employed or struggling to advance in a career, we are definitely in deep water!

The fact is, it is no longer a matter of choice for most women to work outside the home; our economy has adapted to the two-income family. Meanwhile, our natural need for daily renewal is increasingly brushed aside for greater productivity. Beyond hurried moments for personal hygiene, how many of us practice genuine rituals of self-care? We are lucky to get to work on time, get dinner on the table, and later collapse in bed with precious few moments for talk or reading. Then, as we inevitably age and must face new challenges to our health and identity, we are ruthlessly bombarded with an array of youth-oriented skin-care lines, fitness products, and the like. Most of us feel we barely get by day to day, let alone have time to think about rejuvenating ourselves or turning back the clock.

Is there no way out of this dilemma? Before we can realistically discuss the impact of the superwoman syndrome on sexuality, we must realize just how incompatible the two are. In so many varied and complex ways, lack of time to care for oneself greatly diminishes sexual desire.

Yes, there are decent stop-gap measures, such as the weekend getaway, luncheon rendezvous, or private evening out. These do help to maintain a sense of balance by providing escape and relief from tension. But ultimately, snatched moments together are not enough, because real intimacy cannot be staged or forced; it must be based on genuine communication. If communication is continually disrupted or shelved indefinitely, sudden episodes of private time can end up in arguments or long, involved discussions that sap instead of renew. As Margaret reports, "We'd start out with a romantic meal or something, then wild and crazy sex. But when we finally got down to talking, I felt this resentment . . . why do I have to do it all? The day-to-day routine is bad enough, but even on vacation, I'm initiating talks and fielding the upsets. I feel unseen, invisible. I'm taking care of everything and everybody, but nobody cares for me."

TRANSFORMING
SEX-ROLE EXPECTATIONS

Margaret's lament hits it right on the mark for many of us. Unfortunately, the solution isn't any easier to bear than the problem, but here it is: the only one who can really take care of Margaret is Margaret herself. This means revamping priorities so that her own are at the top. Further, her entire sex-role image must be reconditioned from serving others to nurturing herself. This is a drastic shift from what our mothers believed and what society continues to expect of us.

This is especially difficult in that society refuses to accord women equal rights and privileges to those held by men. As a group, men have a higher pay scale, greater social security benefits, more free time, and more opportunity to play. With our role as servant so deeply entrenched in social structure, in the institutions of marriage, education, health care, business, and religion, we are going to have to assert loud and clear just exactly what we need, and how and when we need it. To quote once again the indomitable Camille Paglia, "Feminism begins at home. It begins with every single woman drawing the line."[1]

For years, women were taught to be peacemakers, to soothe and heal, to handle the emotional problems of others to the exclusion of their own. When we behave thus with men, it's no wonder that we find them to be out of touch with their feelings. It is true that men have an inherent difficulty, due to brain structure and function, in linking emotion to other aspects of behavior and response. But why should we go so far as to translate their emotions for them? Perhaps we would find less resentment on their part if we focused our efforts on putting our feelings, needs, and desires forward overtly, rather than covertly. This is a very different model of relationship from the norm, but might serve to create a healthier sort of intimacy.

One woman shared these words from her husband: "You know, you women think you have it so hard, but at least you know what you're fighting for. You've got principles . . . for us guys, if we start to open up and change, it's pretty confusing." Although we may feel compassion for men in this quandary, we must continuously beware of rescuing them. When we do, we perpetuate the problem by colluding with it.

Much has been said of late about women's anger, but what about that of men? Ours is fairly easy to root in inequality, overwork, and unsupportive social structures; in general, we are angry at society. For men, it is different; society is basically supportive and is therefore not the target, but women often are. Rape is an obvious sign of this; violent pornography further serves to illustrate. Men are angry at women for brushing them off, abandoning them to their own confusion, failing to make the pain and frustration of life easier to bear. And it's true that many of us are just too busy to bother with male angst as we once did.

On the other hand, the stress of competing in a man's world has led certain women to adopt male characteristics almost to the near exclusion of their own. So deeply have we rebelled against being stereotyped as weak, indecisive, and irrational that some of us have inadvertently rejected the positive side of these aspects: vulnerability, flexibility, and creativity. True, we have practically been forced to do so to advance in our careers. But perhaps it is time to expand a bit and to reincorporate the more feminine aspects of our personalities into our way of life, our approach to problem solving, and our relationships.

Author John Gray has perceptively described four common male/female patterns of relationship. Of particular relevance here is his description of that in which the woman becomes so independent that she severs critical ties with herself and others. We know her by the following: (1) she is overly defensive; (2) she is compulsively organized and responsible; (3) she is suspicious, cold, and critical; (4) she is pushy and manipulative; (5) she is tense, intolerant, judgmental, and impatient; (6) she is unable to accept support.[2] Not surprisingly, she tends to be partnered to one who is weak, dependent, unfocused. Of course, it is easy to see how many of the brightest and most creative women of our time have wound up this way. But such imbalance is clearly at odds with health and happiness, sexual receptivity and pleasure.

As Stacy relates, "I kept blaming Bob, but I knew it was me. I had become so sharp with him, so on edge all the time, so critical and controlling, that we just didn't get along. I convinced myself that sex was still fine; after all, I knew well enough to let my guard down in bed. But the chemistry between us, the erotic side of our day-to-day contact, was missing."

Accordingly, men who have sought to subdue their masculine traits in deference to the feminine may find themselves less dynamic in their relationships or life in general. Although it's good for men to be open, sensitive, and easygoing at times, chronic confusion, indecisiveness, or irresponsibility are signs of trouble. Particularly when a man begins to live on dreams, or becomes moody and withdrawn much of the time, something is definitely

gone. They states, To whatever extent a partner must suppress their ways of being, feeling, thinking, or doing in order to receive love or be safe in a relationship, the passion will fade."

This is a complex matter and not an easy one to remedy. But in general, women can benefit by recognizing and owning their feminine and masculine traits, and keeping an eye on the balance. Changes in lifestyle, rhythms of activity and rest may be in order. Women of today often need to deliberately evoke the feminine. Sometimes the only way to accomplish this is by breaking routine, perhaps taking a vacation. Dialing and tuning the male and female in oneself can be a lot of fun. To be able to do so is a landmark of maturity, bound to have an enriching effect on sexuality.

But make no mistake—women need intimate relationships in their lives to reflect back meaning and significance. We are so expansive by nature that, as a matter of course, our energies tend to become diffused. Intimate connections with others help us reconnect with ourselves. This links to our tendency to consolidate our understanding of a matter by talking it through with close friends, formulating and evolving thoughts aloud. In *Women's Ways of Knowing*, this unique ability of women to share half-baked truths, in contrast to men's preference for airing already polished positions, was referred to by women themselves as "real talk."[3]

Implicit here is a crucial component of female well-being: the need for the confidences and companionship of other women. It is time for us to acknowledge that we have certain needs readily met by women that are rarely satisfied by men. This is the basis for forming women's groups, organizing circle rituals, and cultivating long-term friendships.

Revamping role expectations carries the liability of loss—loss of identity, of familiar patterns of relating, of sexual intimacy. These losses are usually temporary, but worrisome nonetheless.

Says Susan, "When I started to be truthful with my partner, I was pretty scared. Scared he wouldn't love me, wouldn't care, or even worse, *couldn't* help me. We were both surprised, I think, to find that we kept on going and things began to change. But for a while, we couldn't make love. A lot was being stirred up for both of us."

How to respond to estrangement depends largely on what is causing it, on the underlying issues. Sometimes a couple can handle these on their own; other times, extra support and counseling become necessary. And it may be that patience with one another, via an agreement to "give it some time," will allow for spontaneous resolution.

SEX AND ANGER

On the other hand, if there is deep-seated anger in relationship, sexual intimacy may all but vanish. As expert Marilyn Ruman, Ph.D., says, "Anger is almost always the enemy of desire and is one of the best places to look when your sex life is floundering."[5]

Often couples are not fully aware of how much anger they carry. Typically, one will try to force the other to act the anger out, while taking a turn at resistance and avoidance. These patterns have their roots in a childhood spent with parents doing much the same, enacting extremes of submission and domination. Particularly when chemical dependency, physical abuse, or sexual abuse have been involved, the survivor comes to believe (and rightly so, in such situations) that expressing anger leads to danger and unhappiness.

The shadow side of anger is sadness and loss. If there are long-standing, unresolved traumas such as those cited above, they must be worked through with counseling before there can be any hope for intimacy. But in any relationship in which anger is being repressed, time is of the essence. The longer a couple has been holding back and accumulating resentment, the more each will expect (or try to force) the other to make it up to them. (This is why patterns of d~~~~~ ¹

~ ~~~~~~~ mordinate amounts of time in separate parts of the house, taking meals separately, going to bed at different times, or arguing just before bed are classic examples. Not taking care of oneself physically, neglecting shared environments (particularly the bedroom), or cluttering free time with small talk and housework are other clues. Making changes in these areas, as well as expressing needs to one another regularly (perhaps on a daily basis at first), will get the relationship back on track. If certain patterns of avoidance seem deeply entrenched, it may be necessary to have counseling.

STRESS AND SEXUALITY

Let's backtrack a bit and examine more fully the effects of stress on sexuality. To do so, we must consider the physical effects of stress on the adrenal glands. The adrenals are composed of two parts, the medulla and the cortex. Under stress, the medulla produces catecholamines, one of which is adrenaline, responsible for the flight-or-fight response we feel when threatened or under fire. The cortex produces the sex hormones estrogen and progesterone, but more significantly, the androgens responsible for the libido. To some degree these functions are opposing; if, for example, stress is chronic or protracted so that the medulla must continually pump the body with catecholamines, the production of androgens from the cortex may be neglected. Here we have a physiological explanation of how stress may dampen sexual desire.

Psychologically, stress causes us to withdraw in order to consolidate ourselves, to hold back from sharing with another. Sexual activity under these circumstances simply may not occur, or if it does, it may be brief and fairly explosive (nothing wrong with that, but it doesn't do much on the emotional level, particularly if both partners are under stress). The challenges of unwinding in bed, encountering emotions carefully held in check, or stumbling on outright blocks while trying to coordinate with another person struggling with the same process can be formidable enough to dissuade one from even making the effort. And some couples do fine with nonsexual phases if they keep the communication going in other ways, particularly through shared activities that both enjoy.

Others choose to just have sex, be it good, bad, or indifferent, for the sake of keeping a sense of connection and physical closeness. From Natalie: "It's rough for us right now: we both knock ourselves out at work, the kids get little of our attention, we both feel guilty and angry, and often we take it out on each other. Then we have sex to make up. Sometimes it's great, a real release. Sometimes it just doesn't make it; we're still all bottled up, and we feel more separate than before. But that's marriage, I guess."

Either way, couples suffering from chronic stress will find it an obstacle to intimacy. And the answer lies not in the bedroom but in learning to recognize the problem and handle it intelligently. To complicate matters, men and women generally have different reactions to stress. Whereas men tend to pull back and withdraw to consider the situation objectively, women often respond with a rush of emotion; they need to sift through their feelings and discuss them with someone to find stability. This is how women separate their needs from the needs of others and avoid becoming overwhelmed.

Women who are overwhelmed have one particular characteristic in common: they lose the ability to prioritize.[6] Every task and obligation suddenly assumes equal importance. Whether it's finishing up a project to meet a deadline or folding the laundry, everything is done in a continuous overwrought stream of activity, rather like a runaway train.

When a woman gets more and more removed from her feelings, she is likely to overreact to the inconsequential. Not being conscious of important issues, she will find little irritations and focus her frustration and anger

If stress is due to illness or a crisis involving a loved one or family member, outside support becomes crucial. Even if the situation cannot be altered, at least it can be tempered with understanding and made somewhat tolerable. Again, the media has misled us by overly portraying the happy family, particularly on television; seldom do we see serious crises without immediate resolution, or the protracted stress and agony of losing an intimate friend to terminal illness, addiction, or other destructive behavior (more on this in Chapter 8). Maintaining personal autonomy is the key, for it is the only way to be renewed and thus strong enough to care for another. Beyond support, we need outside activities, structure and routine, and meaningful work to do. Sex may be low on the list of priorities, but it can serve to renew and strengthen us if we but recognize the range of emotions we bring to it.

HOW CHILDREN AFFECT SEXUALITY

Let's look specifically at how having children may affect our sexuality. We will consider some of the key developmental phases in children's lives and how these might affect the inclination for and enjoyment of sex.

T. Berry Brazelton, authority on child rearing and development, notes that as a child reaches the age of two, parents may
begin to compete for his or her affections.[7] If competition or poor
communication exist in other areas of their lives (which is probable, considering how little time parents of a toddler have for
themselves and each other), they may become estranged and dysfunctional as a unit. In other words, for want of privacy and intimacy with one another, parents may transfer their needs onto their
child and begin to vie bitterly for his or her attention.

If this situation is neglected, studies show that the time most
likely for new parents to engage in extramarital affairs is when the
child is three or four. By then, the sheer survival issues of the first
few years have been surmounted and parents have an opportunity
to view the wreckage. Along the way, the tensions of sleep deprivation, continuous interruption, and other stresses have called for
relief, but all too often, parents vent their anger and frustration in
private or may take it out on each other. Thus it may be that by
baby's fourth birthday, parents view each other as less than friends
and sex with an outsider not such a far-fetched idea.

There are things you can do to forestall such a crisis that are
well worth the effort. Consider the following suggestions.

Take Private Time

This is *not* optional! It is the first principle in finding the energy
and enthusiasm for relating to another. One way to do this is to
squeeze time out of your usual routine. For example, timesaving
devices like slow cookers and rice cookers or prewashed salad
greens can simplify meals so much that you have an extra hour
free before dinner. Or you can arrange chores to run simultaneously instead of one by one, saving time and steps. Changing your
standards of order and cleanliness with regard to the house may
also save time and your nerves.

Another more lasting and self-affirming approach is to
change the usual routine so that time for yourself is a natural part
of it. Teach your children, right from the start, how to take care of

themselves. Many of us were brought up by postwar parents who wanted to give us the best of everything, and in truth, they over-did it. We need to create a healthier model whereby every family member does his or her share. This may mean teaching your husband to take care of himself as well as performing his rightful share of household duties. If you are in a position to hire help, *do* it. Save your marriage by keeping hold of yourself.

Housework is a l

, and signed, preferably in blood, by both parties."[8]

Keep Up with Your Dreams

Don't let your dreams get away, or fade so you no longer recognize them. Take time to review your goals in life and fantasies of what could be, giving yourself free rein to be visionary. Where do you want to be a year from now, five, ten? What are the things you feel you absolutely must do in life or you won't really have lived? Some say that whatever you loved to do when you were seven or eight years old holds the key to your future. Think back, dream forward, and keep track.

Make Time for the Relationship

When you are very busy, intimacy must be made a priority if you expect to enjoy it day to day. This means setting aside "couple time"—literally scheduling it in. Maintain a regular date night. And set aside another time, preferably in the morning when you are both fresh, to talk together about what is going on in your lives and how you feel about it. This is a time for open sharing and disclosure, with ground rules of hearing one another out without being judgmental. Some couples do this daily, others once a week, but the more you do it, the more it will tend to occur spontaneously.

Never underestimate the power of an entire night alone together. There is a big difference between sex when you know you might be awakened or interrupted and sex with both total privacy and the freedom to get into it again a little later. Perhaps you have forgotten this, but take my word for it! At least twice a year, you must get away to some romantic and enjoyable location and re-create your love.

Surprise Yourself and Your Lover

In a nutshell, do the unexpected once in a while. When you were courting, a lot of excitement was generated by doing new things together, sharing adventures, discovering mutual reactions to foreign situations. Let this element of excitement back into your life, and don't worry too much about appearing foolish. Take a few risks and try new things, food, clothing, kinds of entertainment, and places to go. Often we marry because we have tired of running around with little or no stability in our lives; we long for a nice, simple routine. But routine is routine; it needs the spice of innovation to keep it from becoming dull. Taking in new impressions is a time-honored way of stimulating creativity and passion. Reanimate!

Get Help If You Need It

Marriage or couple counseling doesn't have to be a long-term proposition. People often end up in counseling because it is the only way they seem able to make the time to talk to one another. As long as there are no serious problems in the marriage such as abuse or violence, counseling can be a simple matter of letting someone more objective observe your process of communication and help you be more personally effective and mutually receptive to one another. From there, new patterns of behavior can be created so that you can discern and solve problems on your own.

Almost every intimate partnership needs a boost like this once in a while.

Another critical time for mothers is when their child begins school full-time or is secondary school age. Clearly, the child is no longer an infant, and all the trappings of that phase come to an end. Between the ages of five and seven, children identify with the family unit; thereafter, they begin to identify with society at large. If a mother has been at home full time ...

... these blues as the height of irrationality. They remember the sleepless nights, the teething, the mad shuffle for babysitters, the interrupted lovemaking, and above all, their partner's complaints, and wonder how she can possibly be serious!

What it really comes down to is reassembling your identity and establishing new goals for yourself and the relationship. Especially for the full-time mom with time on her hands, the questions are tough: what do I do now? Who am I, with my child out of my arms and off to school? Now is the time when recalling your ambitions becomes crucial. Particularly if a woman has given up her career for motherhood and is thinking of going back to it, she must take a hard look at just how far she has fallen behind.

In any period of change, we cling to the past to find courage for the future. We use what we have been as a springboard for what we will become. Listen to what Christine had to say at this juncture: "I was happy Zoe was off to school, but I did feel empty a little, too. Especially with my husband, Jon—I just couldn't make him understand. Really, I didn't understand it myself, until one day it was suddenly clear. Before, when I was recovering from the birth and trying to get my body back, I wanted him to love me for what I was before—to remind me, you know? Now, with Zoe out in the world, I want him to reaffirm me as her mother, love me for that. That I don't *have* to be anything else."

Here again we have an example of a woman wanting reassurance from her partner that she really needs to give herself. The important thing is to see in these feelings the seeds of growth and change, and then respond accordingly.

Another challenging phase for a mother is the onset of her child's adolescence, particularly with a daughter. I recall describing mine at age 11 as being in a perpetual state of PMS. This is also the time when girls typically find fault with their mothers, particularly in the area of personal appearance. I remember coming out dressed for a party one night when my daughter remarked quite caustically, "You're not going to wear *that*, are you?" The stress of the situation is compounded if mom has reached some major chronological landmark of her own, say, her fortieth birthday. In spite of herself, she may end up making expensive trips to the cosmetics counter, beauty salon, or dieters group. Not necessarily bad, all this, but the upshot may be marked and persistent uncertainty about her physical attributes and basic sex appeal.

This is further complicated by the natural shift in power that occurs in adolescence. Particularly if your style has been strictly to enforce your will on your young ones, their natural rebellion at this age can leave you feeling utterly powerless. And in truth, the role of parent does begin to change from guardian to guide and confidant. As the bread-baking theory of child rearing goes, you mix and add ingredients when children are young, you watch the dough rise (and must deflate it occasionally) as they mature, but once in the oven of adolescence, you had better not open the door! Yes, you keep an eye on things, but you don't interfere unless the bread is about to burn. If, however, a woman is herself in upheaval with midlife reassessment, she is likely to struggle with this shift more than usual and take it as yet another blow to her already fragile self-confidence. This may merit a call to a counselor or support network of some kind.

THE MIDLIFE TURNAROUND

Superwomen and supermoms come in all ages. But depending on the decade of a woman's life, she will have particular sexual needs and orientation. Sex in young adulthood is largely about identifying with and pleasing another. Sex in the thirties tends to focus on pair-bonding and procreation. Sex in midlife reestablishes the priorities of the self: physical, emotional, and spiritual. T-l:-- -¹ ¹------¹ ·   ·

My husband had affairs from the time he turned 40, and I only found out three years later. I was so furious, so humiliated that I really didn't think we were going to make it. Couldn't sleep with him at all, but he wanted to stay so we had counseling. All that stuff, I'll spare you—but when we finally started making love again, I was a different women. I went out for myself. Whenever the pain of his betrayal would start to get to me, I'd hold on to myself and just do what I felt was best for me. I got in touch with a strength I didn't know I had before, and I aligned myself with it, even in bed.

Of course, there are many women who choose with all good reason to cut their losses on pain like this and move on. Some have affairs of their own, in search of healing. Others become obsessed with their attractiveness, doing almost anything to stay young. But that which Barbara called aligning with her strength is increasingly crucial for us as we mature; it enables us to meet challenges to our health and mobility as we age. Is it not fitting that in midlife, we should seek to explore and express ourselves as never before? "Forty and fabulous": we know what we like, we speak our minds, we have a solid base from which to innovate, and pleasure is ours for the taking!

Here's an interesting comment from a friend several weeks after her fortieth birthday: "I thought midlife crises were only for men. But it's really hit me. I'm turning into a real loud mouth, saying things to my boss and husband I wouldn't have *dreamed* of saying before! You figure you have only so much time . . . I feel almost ruthless about getting my needs met."

And what was this doing to her sex life? "This is pretty personal, but in the middle of making love one night I just blurted out, "Joe, why don't you *concentrate?*' I never said anything like that before . . . see, my husband just tends to ramble on sometimes in bed, without focusing on me. When he paused (I guess he was a little shocked), I added, 'You know, concentrate on me.' I couldn't believe I did that!"

It is a well-known fact that whereas men reach their sexual peak (as per intensity and endurance) in their early twenties, women reach theirs later, often in their forties. This is partly physical, partly psychological. For many women, it takes that long to get to know themselves sexually, to overcome taboos of sexual self-expression, to come to know and trust their bodies, and to be confident enough to let go and get what they want in bed.

This is also a time when women who have never fantasized before find their sexual imaginations coming to life. In her book *Women on Top*, author Nancy Friday makes clear both the range and outrageousness of women's sexual fantasies as they reach this peak. Interestingly, these fantasies are quite physically oriented, focused on ways of maximizing sensation, while the fantasies of younger women are more emotionally based. For example, the woman in her twenties might fantasize about a romantic buildup and tender preludes to intercourse, whereas the midlife woman focuses more on positions, techniques of her partner, or even on bondage and multiple partners as enhancements to her sensation.

June Reinisch, in the Kinsey Report, notes that men and women do a turnaround in sexual temperament about this time. As women become more physically oriented and intrigued with physical experimentation, men become interested in letting themselves be vulnerable and caring.[9] These changes are, in fact, hormonally based, for as women approach menopause, their reproductive hormones may surge intensely to force ovulation. Thus women tracking their cycles commonly report month-to-month fluctuations in their fertility, with ovulation so intense that, as one woman put it, "fertile mucus runs down ......

.... to be, emotionally and romantically. Yes, this strikes women in their forties as the height of irony: all those years they yearned for romance, while he wanted nothing but sex! The trick is to turn these facts of life to one's advantage (which some women do by forming liaisons with younger men).

Androgen and testosterone levels do, in fact, correlate to degree of aggressiveness in women and, in many instances, inclination to stay in monogamous relationships. According to a study conducted by Patricia Schreiner-Engel, associate professor of gynecology/obstetrics and psychiatry at Mount Sinai School of Medicine in New York City, women in the most powerful career positions had the highest testosterone levels. "They were more achievement-oriented. One was the head of a nursing union; another was an importer. Almost none of them was in an ongoing long-term relationship. On the other hand, women on the lower end of the range were homemakers, students, or temporary workers, but they had enduring marriages."

Of course, cultural and socioeconomic factors affect these findings considerably. But something very important, and heretofore overlooked, can be extrapolated from this research as regards women in midlife. If it is true that at this stage *all* women experience the effects of skyrocketing testosterone linked to urges for independence, there must be some correlation between peak levels of this hormone and midlife crisis, not to mention the high divorce rate among couples in their forties.

All the more reason, then, for recasting sex roles and experimenting a little. Most likely to interfere with this endeavor are overwork and overextension. Outright polarization will occur in relationships if there is no give and take, if both partners feel their new sexual needs to be unmet.

Says Laurie, "At first, I thought there was something wrong with my partner, that he was slowing down, losing his grip for some physical reason. This happened about the same time I seemed to want sex to be more physically forceful than before: faster, rougher. I found myself getting impatient with Ken, wishing he'd get on with it, at the same time feeling like a heel for being so pushy and demanding. But damn, what I wanted felt right to me, and I didn't want to put on the brakes."

This is a good start; the feeling is genuine and it fits with the natural shift. But there will be a breakdown here without frank communication, understanding, and mutual support. If he wants to take more time warming up, choose your favorite foreplay and spell it out, loud and clear. If he is pacing himself to the utmost, initiate changes in position that keep the stimulation level high enough for you. Bring your fantasies into the picture somehow. And don't be surprised if he is the one wanting afterglow cuddling and pillow talk!

The positive side of these changes is illustrated by these words from Candace: "We'd been together for 12 years, and I finally felt like our sex life was really on track. We truly understood where the other was coming from, because we'd each pretty much been there ourselves—we'd run the gamut, I guess! Sex just got better and better, and we had an ongoing sexual dimension in our communication that I remembered from the early stages of our relationship. It surprised me, exceeded my expectations, and was well worth waiting for."

This may also be a point when women seek relationships with other women for the first time, finding both personal and worldly egalitarianism. As Lynn reports, "I never considered myself bisexual, never thought of being with a woman until I reached a place of certainty and confidence in myself that made me long for the affinity of an equal. I'd been with so many men, struggling with their problems. Then I fell in love with Susan, and found common life experience, humor, flexibility, and passion perfect for this time of my life."

1. Camille Paglia, "Hurricane Camille Wreaks Havoc," *San Francisco Chronicle* (Sept. 1992).

2. John Gray, *Men, Women and Relationships* (Hillsboro, Or: Beyond Words Publishing, 1990).

3. M.F. Belenky, B.M. Clinchy, N.R. Goldberg, and J.M. Tarule, *Women's Ways of Knowing* (New York: Basic Books, 1986).

4. Ibid.

5. Marilyn Ruman, *New Woman* (April 1991).

6. Gray, *Men, Women and Relationships*.

7. T. Berry Brazelton, *Infants and Mothers* (New York: Delacorte Press, 1969).

8. Andrew Ward, *Out Here* (New York: Penguin Books, 1991).

9. June Reinisch, "The Kinsey Report" (syndicated), *San Francisco Chronicle* (1990).

6

Menopause ~~ 1 ~

...age sig-
...that causes distress, it's the process itself, with
its tempestuous and uncontrollable physical and emotional side
effects. Who has time for all that, in the midst of family obligations and a career most likely at its peak? How are we to cope, for
example, with the disruption and embarrassment of hot flashes in
the middle of an important presentation or social occasion? And
how do we handle the distress of vaginal dryness when we really
want to make love?

Add to these difficulties an array of cultural bias against aging, particularly for women, who often find themselves bereft of
identity as they grow older, and it's no wonder we approach menopause with a sense of dread. But there are other ways to view the
process that accord women greater dignity and self-respect so that
the benefits of this phase, not the least of which are sexual, may be
readily recognized and enjoyed.

WHAT IS MENOPAUSE?

Beyond the obvious cessation of menstruation are the underlying
causes of menopause. At puberty, a girl has approximately 300,000
follicles, or egg-forming cells, whereas a woman approaching

menopause has only 8,000 or so remaining. The eggs are destroyed
by a combination of stress, radiation (via sun exposure), or natural
degeneration according to built-in lifespan. As the eggs diminish
in number, ovulation may not occur. And unless an egg ripens,
there will be no corpus luteum to release progesterone. Despite the
fact that the pituitary tries to compensate with extra surges of FSH
and LH, the ovaries become less and less responsive and their
production of estrogen eventually ceases.

Menopause occurs on average between the ages of 48 and 52,
but some women stop menstruating as early as their late thirties.
And before the periods actually cease there are four to six years
when hormone levels progressively decline. Thus menopause may
be divided into two phases: premenopausal and menopausal. Pre-
menopause is characterized by sharp fluctuations in levels of progesterone (estrogen diminishes steadily, whereas if no egg ripens in
a particular cycle, progesterone will drop abruptly). This leads to
sporadic bleeding, and changes in cycle length and amount of
bleeding with menstruation. Commonly, periods come closer together and become much heavier; bleeding for a week to ten days
is not unusual.

Problems can occur if blood loss is extreme, if bleeding lasts
further into the cycle, or if cumulative blood loss becomes excessive. Sometimes a D and C is done in these cases, and cells from
the uterus are checked for any sign of abnormality. Cancer, polyps,
and fibroid growths are possible causes, and can thus be ruled out.
But most of the time, the problem is simply that progesterone
levels are not adequate to maintain the uterine lining. Changes in
diet and lifestyle, along with herbal remedies, may be of benefit.
Studies have shown that deficiencies of iron, vitamin C, and
bioflavonoids can exacerbate heavy bleeding. Cigarette smoking,
stress, and excessive intake of alcohol can also contribute to the
problem.

Some women have little trouble with progesterone-related
symptoms and notice only that their periods are coming less often
and are becoming lighter. This is when the well-known symptoms
of menopause—the hot flashes, mood swings, night sweats, and

vaginal changes—come into play. About 80 percent of women experience some of these symptoms while passing through menopause.

When a woman has stopped menstruating for a full year, menopause is considered to be complete. The age at which menopause occurs is somewhat hereditary; if a woman's mother or sisters were early or late, she is likely to follow suit. For whatever reason, women in industrialized countries are experiencing men----[1]

...what will this last third of her life be like? Is she doomed, as the media would generally have us believe, to be shriveled and sexless—a doddery "senior citizen"? That depends largely on how well she takes care of herself and how she defines herself socially and individually. But first, she must find a way to make it through "the change."

Male authorities on the subject have been little more than harbingers of doom. Robert A. Wilson, author of *Feminine Forever* and staunch advocate of hormone replacement therapy (HRT), describes menopause as "the loss of womanhood and the loss of good health," claiming that chemical imbalance results in "castration" and a state of "living decay."[1] David Reuben, author of *Everything You Always Wanted to Know About Sex but Were Afraid to Ask*, summarily expresses the antiquated view of menopause as the end point for women: "Having outlived their ovaries, they may have outlived their usefulness as human beings. The remaining years may just be marking time until they follow their glands into oblivion."[2] Sheila Kitzinger, on the other hand, sees menopausal changes as those by which "a new balance is found, one which is natural and right for an older woman," through a process she likens to adolescence.[3] She is quick to point out that although estrogen and progesterone diminish greatly, they are counterbalanced by the hormone testosterone. Susan Lark, author of *The Menopause Self-Help Book*, notes that many women pay better attention to their diet and lifestyle during menopause, so that these years become exciting and enriching, a time of "vigor and vitality."[4]

The key, I think, is to view menopause as a natural transition, but a transition nonetheless. In other words, it is a period of intense and incontrovertible change, marked by extremes. And, as is true of the transition phase of childbirth or the premenstrual phase of the monthly cycle, success is found not in trying to take charge or get control of the situation but by cooperating with it, seeing it through. Premenstrually or in labor, there are specific coping techniques for dealing with physical and emotional difficulties; the same is true in menopause. But beyond all this, trust in the process as natural, positive, and nonthreatening will be the determining factor in the ease of its progression, the triumph in its completion, and the insight gleaned along the way.

Our culture places so great a premium on feminine constancy that women are often denied the right to experience the heights and depths of life, as men do by acts of daring and bravado, creativity and delusion, rebellion and peace. For women, the ability to know these things is there in the flesh, patterned hormonally in a sequence that repeatedly comes full circle and gives meaning and continuity to life. But certain phases are undeniably tumultuous and extreme.

Characteristic of any period of transition is the chance to take stock, to assess where we have been and where we have yet to go. Typical midlife comments like, "I haven't accomplished what I hoped in my career," or, "I feel unfulfilled in my primary relationships," hold keys for formulating new plans. Sweeping changes can, and probably should, occur at this time. A third of one's life yet to be lived is quite a long time, especially with the benefit of experience. It would be foolish not to use this transition for a few radical departures and explorations into the unknown.

And, in this regard, it is probable that anything we cling to that needs to be released will tend to make menopause worse.

Women now have lives outside the home, and for the most part, are having children later than ever before. Surely it is not easy to go through menopause when your children are struggling with adolescence, but it must be even harder if they have recently left home and you are utterly at a loss for what to do. In my research, I have found that the main thing menopausal women share is an emphasis on letting go, carrying on, finding new work to do, new ways to get more out of life.

There is no direct

.... what

..........ation of what to do about it. It seems clear that decreased estrogen and increased testosterone coincide with menopausal women's need for self-assertion.

PHYSICAL SYMPTOMS AND TREATMENT

Many symptoms of menopause are autonomic, such as hot flashes, sweating, heart palpitations, and itching of the skin. Others are physical or metabolic, such as vaginal dryness, bladder dysfunction, bone thinning (osteoporosis), joint pain, muscular weakness, shrinking and sagging of the breasts, skin drying and wrinkling, thinning of the hair, weight gain, and periodic complaints of bloating and headache. Emotional symptoms include moodiness, irritability, insomnia, forgetfulness, and changes in sexual function or desire. Approaches to dealing with these symptoms fall basically into two camps: one, of obliteration through hormonal control; two, of cooperation by way of health-enhancing natural practices and methods of response.

Hormone replacement treatment was the brainchild of physicians (such as the aforementioned Wilson) who perceived menopause, along with childbearing and menstruation, as little more than a disease requiring medication. An interesting aside that serves as an illustration: one of my students recounted how her mother, in giving birth to her, had called the doctor a "goddamn son-of-a-bitch" at the height of transition, and was promptly sedated. Let's face it: most men feel more than a little threatened in the midst of biological transitions, particularly when at full throttle, and have long sought ways to dominate and control women at these junctures. Medication is a powerful way to do this. This is not to discount the value of and need for hormone replacement in certain circumstances, but the routine use of hormones to address common complaints of menopause is just as bad as drugging the body in childbirth or obliterating premenstrual symptoms with sedatives. HRT was, in fact, touted as the only way menopausal women might hope to stay youthful; in the 1960s, it was considered a panacea for sleeplessness, depression, loss of interest in sex, dry skin and hair, fatigue—in other words, all the undesired effects of aging.

Although estrogen replacement can have a positive effect on hot flashes, vaginal changes, and osteoporosis, it has serious side effects and contraindications. The risk of uterine cancer is ten times higher in menopausal women using estrogen, particularly if taken alone. It is now generally combined with progesterone to lessen this risk. However, despite the mix, breast cancer rates are four times higher than normal for women using this therapy for six years or more.[5] Estrogen therapy is also known to increase the risk of gall bladder disease, thrombosis, phlebitis, headaches, and depression. It is contraindicated for anyone suffering from liver disease, sickle cell anemia, gall stones, diabetes, or undiagnosed abnormal vaginal bleeding.

Side effects of excess estrogen include salt and water retention, folic acid anemia, bloating, nausea, and breast tenderness. Progesterone (given as progestins) can increase susceptibility to vaginal yeast and other infections, fatigue, and hirsutism (excess body and facial hair).

Sedatives and tranquilizers are also prescribed for menopausal women, and sometimes added to the estrogen formula. This makes sense, in a way, because one of the side effects of HRT is depression. But recent studies have shown that women experiencing menopause are no more inherently depressed than women at other stages of life. Rosetta Reitz, author of *Menopause: A Positive Approach*, feels that tranquilizers are prescribed primarily to keep menopausal women out of sight and out of mind and conjectures: "Do you know what would happen if all the women between 40 and 55 started making demands? My adrenaline begins to burst forth at the excitement of the idea."[6] Tranquilizers are also addic

tomy. Compared to women taking the usual HRT formula, those with added testosterone had more intense sexual desires and fantasies, were more easily aroused, and had orgasms more frequently. They also had higher energy levels and a greater sense of well-being.

Herbs such as nettle stimulate the adrenals to produce adequate testosterone. Red raspberry leaf and hawthorne berry teas invigorate the system and may alleviate depression. As we look more closely at the impact certain symptoms of menopause have on sexuality, we will consider the pros and cons of HRT plus the benefits of herbs, supplements, and dietary changes. (For more detailed information, see the charts on pages 132 and 136–37.)

Now, let's look more closely at some of the major symptoms of menopause, particularly those that might affect sexuality, and consider the pros and cons of HRT, plus the benefits of herbs, supplements, and dietary changes.

Hot Flashes

Three out of four women experience hot flashes; they are the most common menopausal symptom. And this symptom is the only one that is universal, occurring among women in nearly every culture.

During a hot flash, a woman experiences a rush of heat to her chest, neck, and face, or sometimes throughout her body. This can happen anytime, anywhere. The skin flashes, temperature increases, and breathing becomes shallow. There may also be an itching sensation. As the heat passes, women often find themselves drenched in sweat, and then feel chilly and drained. These episodes may or may not be noticed by others, but most women feel deeply embarrassed by them, lest this declaration of their menopausal condition be made public. In truth, hot flashes make women painfully aware of the social conditioning that undervalues advancing age, which of course only adds to the discomfort.

Physically, hot flashes result from vasomotor instability. They originate in the temperature regulating center of the hypothalamus, and some women find that almost anything that affects temperature, such as exercise, stress, entering a cold or hot room, or even sexual arousal, can trigger a hot flash. Many women also note a strong correlation between drinking caffeinated beverages or alcohol and the onset of hot flashes. Large doses of niacin (vitamin B6) and certain drugs, such as those used to treat hypertension, are implicated. Emotional upsets can trigger hot flashes, too.

Hot flashes were once thought to be due to excess estrogen but are now linked to the very high levels of LH common in menopause. However, the precise mechanism of their occurrence remains unknown.

Some women never experience hot flashes; others have them two and three times a day. Many find they only occur at night. In fact, night sweats during menopause are very much like those postpartum, which are likewise due to hormonal change and fluctuation. Hot flashes should persist for no more than five years; the majority of women have them for several months only.

Common sense measures include layering clothing so that certain items can be shed quickly, keeping a spray bottle by the bed, in the car, or at the office, having a change of sheets or towel by the bed, and using a small electric fan when feasible. Estrogen therapy is sometimes recommended and works fairly well—but the hot flashes come right back when treatment is stopped. Tincture of motherwort, 20 drops under the tongue, is reputed to be one of the best natural remedies. Bioflavonoids added to the diet or taken as a supplement help tremendously. Homeopathic remedies may also be useful, lachesis in particular. (For more information on this and other therapies, see *Menopausal Years: The Wise Woman Way* by Susun Weed. This is a comprehensive and inspiring book; one of my favorites.[7])

Apart from the nuisance, hot flashes may provide an oppor-

...... as crone. that of reaper and transformer. Perhaps hot flashes provide a metaphysical opportunity to get in touch with the shadowy side of one's nature and make peace with it.

Women also find that the more aware they become of the hormonal course during menopause, the more likely they are to know a hot flash is coming. Sometimes revelations may precede the flashes and thus serve as signals to take off a sweater or turn on the fan. After all, hot flashes are symptoms of overload on the endocrine system, which is in the process of adjusting multiple physiological functions to match changed levels of estrogen and progesterone. Overload equals altered state, and that is exactly what hot flashes represent or initiate.[9]

Kitzinger likens the process of coping with hot flashes to that of coping with contractions. She recommends breathing from low in the body—down in the pelvis slowing down and opening up. The overall effect is somewhat erotic, right down to the rosy glow that colors a woman's face and softens her demeanor during arousal. We can use hot flashes to experience heightened awareness in a variety of ways, depending on how we focus our attention.

Just as when we try to recall our dreams and find we must write them down, there is similar benefit in recording the nature,

SYMPTOMS AND TREATMENTS IN MENOPAUSE

	Nutritional Supplements	Natural Sources
Excess bleeding	Vitamin A 5,000 IU	Hawthorn berry
		Vitex
	Vitamin C 1,000 mg	Dandelion root
	Iron 30 mg	Shepherd's purse
	Bioflavonoids 800 mg	Black haw
		False unicorn
		Sarsaparilla
		Wild yam root
Hot flashes	Vitamin E 800 IU	Motherwort
	Bioflavonoids 800 mg	Dong quoi
		Black cohosh
		Fennel
		Pomegranate
Vaginal changes	Vitamin E 800 IU	Motherwort
	Bioflavonoids 800 mg	Saw palmetto berries
	Evening primrose oil	Comfrey ointment
	Linseed oil	
Urinary tract problems	Vitamin C 1,000–1,500 mg	Uva ursi
		Nettle
		Goldenseal
		Black currant
		Yarrow
Osteoporosis	Vitamin D 5,000 IU	Oat straw
	Calcium citrate 1,500 mg	Nettle
	Folic acid 800 mcg	Comfrey root
	Zinc 20 mg	Horsetail
	Magnesium 500 mg	
Nervous irritability	Vitamin B complex 50 mg	Passionflower
	Vitamin C 1,000 mg	Valerian root
	Bioflavonoids 800 mg	Hops
		Catnip
Fatigue, depression	Vitamin B complex 50 mg	Ginger
	Vitamin C 1,000 mg	Cayenne pepper
	Magnesium 500 mg	Oat straw
	Potassium aspartate 100 mg	Blessed thistle

occurrence, and message (if any) in hot flashes. Raskin describes many of her flashes as cryptic enough that she can only decipher their meaning while they are still fresh. Then again, if this seems like unnecessary fuss over a simple and natural function, the sit-back-and-relax approach works just as well!

Vaginal and Pelvic Changes

Besides the aforementioned vaginal d

_ _... ...nce more vulnerable to infection. Decreased estrogen also leads to reduced vaginal and pelvic circulation, implicating the bladder and accounting for the increased incidence of urinary tract infections.

Of all the symptoms of menopause for which estrogen therapy is recommended, vaginal dryness is the one for which it is most widely used. Estrogen is readily absorbed by vaginal tissues, and a single course of cream applied by plunger can sometimes turn things around significantly. Lubricating jelly will still be necessary (vitamin E might be used alternatively). Seminal fluid has a positive effect on vaginal tissues, as does evening primrose oil; both contain prostaglandins, which soften and condition. And orgasm itself is most beneficial: it stimulates circulation and the release of natural, soothing lubrication. According to Reitz, regular intercourse (and masturbation) makes vaginal and pelvic changes at menopause "hardly noticeable." In fact, one study showed that weekly intercourse so increased women's estrogen levels that many common complaints were alleviated.[9]

Continued use of estrogen alone greatly increases the risk of uterine cancer, therefore natural alternatives should be tried and utilized whenever possible. Vitamin E may also be taken supple-

mentally, at least 600 IU daily. Bioflavonoids are remarkably effective for this problem; take approximately 800 mg daily (food sources
include citrus fruits, especially the inner rind, and buckwheat,
which is delicious in pancakes). Herbal teas of licorice root and
black cohosh root also help by stimulating production of estrogen.

With regard to urinary tract problems, herbs like goldenseal
and uva ursi (bearberry) are classic. Goldenseal contains berberine,
which has antibiotic affects, and uva ursi has arbutin, a diuretic
and anti-infective agent. The two can be combined and simmered
slowly for tea, or taken as tincture. See the chart on pages 136–37
for additional ideas.

Osteoporosis

Osteoporosis refers to loss of bone mass, and although it occurs in
men too, it is more common in our culture among women. It is
linked to menopause in that estrogen plays an important role in
maintaining the structure and calcification of bone, thus a decline
in this hormone is thought to precipitate the condition. There are
other factors, however. Genetic predisposition figures strongly in
osteoporosis, as does a diet high in salt, animal protein, caffeine,
alcohol, or carbonated drinks (the excess level of phosphorus directly decreases bone mass). Some authorities feel that inadequate
vitamin D intake, particularly as exposure to sunlight is increasingly discouraged, may be a major, if not primary, factor. This is
corroborated by cross-cultural studies that show osteoporosis as far
from universal in menopausal women. Some populations show no
osteoporosis in women at any age, while in others both men and
women are affected, even prior to midlife. The incidence is definitely higher in industrialized countries, among women who
smoke, those with a Northern European background, those who
are sedentary, and those who regularly use drugs such as steroids,
diuretics, aluminum-containing antacids, thyroid supplements, and
anticonvulsant drugs.

The effects of osteoporosis are worse than the condition itself. The spine tends to compress and curve, and certain bones,

particularly the hips, become highly susceptible to fracture. Such injuries usually occur later, in a woman's seventies or eighties. But 30 percent of women thus affected die of complications, and many more suffer chronic disability.

It seems obvious that diet and lifestyle are major factors in osteoporosis. What are some of the ways women can help prevent this condition from developing? For one thing, they must stop fretting about their weight and concentrate ~ ~

                                                          ~~~~~y of leafy
green vegetables, complex carbohydrates, low-fat foods, and minimal amounts of animal protein (except fish from unpolluted waters). Especially important are trace minerals, those elements leached from the soil by commercial farming methods. Organic fruits and vegetables are sometimes as much as five times higher in food value than their commercial counterparts. It is definitely worth finding a store that stocks organic produce.[10] See the box on page 136–37 for more details on nutrition in menopause.

And then there is lifestyle to consider. Most of us spend way too much time indoors, sitting at a desk or busy with housework that keeps us just this side of aerobic, tense with the pressure of having so many things to do. This is diametrically opposed to what our lives should be about: good food, exercise, and relaxation in complementary measure. In fact, next to getting adequate calcium in the diet, the single most important way to avoid osteoporosis is with plenty of weight-bearing exercise (upright activities such as walking, dancing, lifting light weights, bicycling, and climbing stairs). Remember that women are especially apt to deprive themselves of health-promoting necessities as they defer to the needs of others. Eventually, and sometimes with surprising swiftness, this can catch up with us.

Once again, the message is clear: menopause is a time for realignment. And rather than wait until the time is upon us, we should begin to pay better attention to our health and well-being straight away.

In her bestseller *The Silent Passage*, Gail Sheehy portrays the common complaints of menopause as universally disruptive and virtually incapacitating. And yet, numerous studies show that most

NUTRITION IN MENOPAUSE

Good nutrition is of utmost importance during menopause. As body systems slow down, we must adapt accordingly. The digestive tract produces fewer enzymes and less hydrochloric acid as we age. Yet, many menopausal problems and complaints can be minimized or alleviated by eating the right foods.

Whole grains These include rice, corn, wheat, barley, oats, rye, millet, buckwheat, brown rice, and wild rice. These stabilize blood-sugar levels and can reduce sugar cravings. They help prevent diabetes and may also protect against cancer of the colon as they are high in fiber. Eat freely of these, and aim for some variety each week.

Legumes Legumes are various kinds of peas and beans, such as lentils, kidney beans, black beans, chickpeas, pinto beans, white beans, and split peas. They are very high in protein and fiber, and digest slowly, making them especially appropriate for older women. Problems with gas can be alleviated by slow and thorough cooking, or by eating small amounts.

Vegetables These provide a full range of vitamins and minerals. The dark green, orange, and red varieties are high in vitamin A, which has been shown to protect against cancer of the breast and cervix, as well as immunological disease. Vitamin C has similar benefits and helps prevent excessive bleeding at menopause if combined with iron and bioflavonoids. Good sources of vitamin C include peppers, potatoes, tomatoes, broccoli, cabbage, peas, parsley, and kale. Vegetables also provide important minerals like calcium, magnesium, iron, and trace elements if grown organically. Onions and garlic help lower serum cholesterol, which reduces the risk of strokes and heart attacks. Seaweeds like kelp are high in iodine, which promotes healthy thyroid function.

Fruits Fruits also provide a wide range of vitamins and minerals. They are particularly high in potassium, which serves to regulate blood pressure. Potassium also helps prevent fatigue associated with menopause. Especially rich sources include bananas, berries, melons, grapefruit, peaches, and apricots. High fiber is another bonus because it can minimize constipation. Pineapple and papaya specifically aid digestion by breaking down proteins.

Seeds and nuts These are good sources of protein, but are very high in fat and calories and thus should be eaten sparingly. M-
and calcium are ...

... . (this may also be
.. ..y as linseed oil or in capsules).

Foods to avoid include the following:

Salt In excess, this mineral can exacerbate bloating, high blood pressure, heart disease, and osteoporosis.

Sugar Too much sugar can accelerate diabetes, deplete essential vitamins and minerals, and cause stress, anxiety, and vulnerability to infection.

Caffeine Excess caffeine can cause mood swings, interfere with carbohydrate metabolism, exacerbate hot flashes, and worsen osteoporosis.

Alcohol Alcohol has similar effects to those of caffeine. It also disrupts the liver's ability to metabolize hormones, intensifying menopausal complaints.

Fats Saturated fats, found in dairy products and meats, are especially bad for menopausal women in that they link to heart disease, high blood pressure, stroke, and cancer of the ovaries, breasts, and uterus.

Adapted from *The Menopause Self-Help Book* by Susan Lark, M.D. (Berkeley, Calif.: Celestial Arts, 1990).

women have very little trouble. Often, fear intensifies or exacerbates initial symptoms just enough to drive women to seek hormone replacement, much as fear in labor makes contractions infinitely harder to handle and leads women to ask for drugs. Ask your own mother or older sisters what menopause was like for them, as patterns and severity of symptoms tend to run in families. Even more important are the coping mechanisms your female relations used: what worked and what didn't. I was relieved when my mother told me that menopause had been a breeze for her; she had had hot flashes at night occasionally, and that was about it. If, however, your mother responds with a horror story, don't panic. Get the entire picture, complete with medical interventions, and add lifestyle factors too before jumping to any conclusions.

SEX DURING MENOPAUSE

What's sex like at this time? Reports range wildly, with everything from blooming desire to total disinterest. From Marjorie:

> Looking back, I think my moods had a lot to do with it. I never really let go of having a second child, even though the years went by and nothing happened. Then menopause put an end to that dream, and I cried and raged at my husband, to the point that *he* called the doctor for sedatives! I tried estrogen for a while but just got more depressed. I wanted absolutely nothing to do with Blake . . . I acted as though I blamed him for everything. Actually, I guess I did: when I wanted kids early in our marriage, he wasn't ready, and then we had to wait so long for our son. Anyway, my hot flashes were awful, they happened to me everywhere and often made me cry. Sometimes I'd come home and scream in the closet, when no one was there.
>
> We didn't have sex, except once in a while when I felt I could stomach it, like once a month or so. After it [menopause] was all over, though, I got my drive back all right . . . I

only wish my husband had. Things are different between us
and I know we'll never be the same.

Quite the opposite experience, from Geri:

Menopause was liberation for me. I didn't expect it, but so it
was. No more worry about birth control . . . after four children, free at last! And by then, the ~~~~~~~~

Geri's story is actually a bit more postmenopausal. Here is
Elaine's tale, from deep in the thick of it:

I welcomed menopause; I wasn't afraid because I'd learned to
trust my body over the years and felt ready for whatever it
had in store for me. The intensity of the hot flashes threw
me at first, but I began to see them as a sort of energy
release. When I looked at menopause as a transition to my
wiser, seasoned self, I decided that with every flash, I'd let
something go—some obligation to someone else's priorities,
some outdated idea of myself, some old wound. It was exhilarating to do this—really a rush! Sometimes I'd flash during
intercourse, usually at the beginning of arousal, and I'd use
the energy as sort of a boost to my passion. My partner had
no complaints. He didn't always know what was happening,
but I think it took the edge off my sharpness at times. Menopausal women are so powerful—I think men can be inti-
mated by the change. For us, sex was the bridge.

Diane says of her experience with Elsa:

I was in menopause before my partner, by about a year or so. So we both experienced hot flashes over a period of time, although hers were the most intense. It was fun, really . . . wonderful to have genuine support and understanding. The minor inconveniences some women speak of, like vaginal dryness—well, applying oils to each other became a special part of our sexual pleasure.

And lastly, a classical mixed response:

I grieved during menopause—I hate to admit it, because I consider myself a liberated woman. But who wants to grow old? What woman wants to lose her looks? This deeply affected my self-confidence and desire for sex. I was afraid I'd lose my partner, and so was scared to be vulnerable in bed. When the hot flashes were most intense, a period of three months or so, we stopped making love. My vagina felt different too, dry and very tender. In retrospect, I think I was testing my partner, and lo and behold, after it was all over, he was still there. Then my desire skyrocketed, and I took hold of the situation.

Thus far, we've considered menopause only as a natural phenomenon. When it is surgically induced, as by hysterectomy, the experience is entirely different. Instead of a gradual decline in hormonal levels, the system is thrown into shock and withdrawal.

In 1987, 800,000 American women had hysterectomies, and up to one-third of the surgeries have been called unnecessary. "American women are up to four times more likely to have hysterectomies than women of other industrialized countries."[11] In the UK, one out of five women who reach 75 will have had their uterus removed.[12] Although some doctors truly feel that women not intending to have children and at risk from pelvic diseases are safer without their reproductive organs, such a view totally discounts the physical difficulties and emotional trauma women tend to experience when this transition occurs so abruptly. Even when there are clear indications for surgery, loss of her reproductive organs can cause a woman to sink into depression and undergo a classic process of grieving (see Chapter 8).

There are four general indications for hysterectomy: (1) cancer of the reproductive organs; (2) severe infection of the fallopian tubes, uterus, or ovaries that cannot be controlled; (3) extremely large fibroid tumors; (4) uncontrollable uterine bleeding sive to D and C or any oth

conduction. And if the difficulty is fibroids alone, a myomectomy permits surgical removal of the fibroid while saving the uterus. Although fibroid tissue tends to grow back, myomectomy is the best solution for a woman whose fibroid has grown cumbersome (they can reach a weight of 100 pounds) and who still wants children.

Sex for the woman who has undergone complete hysterectomy is apt to be distressing both physically and emotionally. Annette recalls: "I felt empty, like I had nothing to offer anymore. My muscles were all shot and soft—my vagina was foreign territory to me and I wasn't sure I wanted to get to know it again. To have to face the fact that I'd never have a child and would never give birth was unspeakably painful to me, and wiped the magic from sex and my body for a very long time." Another woman reports: "The inside of me felt all stopped up and rigid—like a dead-end, literally. I had periodic bleeding at first, which was normal, they said. Even though it was scary, I welcomed it—at least *something* was coming out of me! When I bled, I found that I could cry. After it stopped, I turned my sadness inward until I healed."

On the other side, here's an account from Mandy: "I had suffered so tremendously with endometriosis and uterine infection that the decision for hysterectomy came as a relief. I wasn't sure I wanted kids anyway, and now the matter was settled. But I noticed a funny thing: for months after the surgery, I still felt a rhythm, a ghost cycle of sorts. I didn't know how much that rhythm had become a part of me, wracked with pain as I was."

Some women notice a change in orgasms after hysterectomy. The deeper contractions felt in the uterus, or the stimulation of the cervix that some women find pleasurable, are no longer part of the picture. This sort of sexual crisis necessitates refocusing and reconditioning oneself to find satisfaction in other pleasure centers. With abrupt withdrawal of estrogen, even the clitoris may atrophy, but ongoing stimulation via masturbation generally serves to compensate.

Sometimes, though, symptoms of surgically induced menopause are so severe as to necessitate HRT, at least for a time. Many women try to taper the hormones down to a minimal level by their late forties, and discontinue them in their fifties. Others choose to stay on them indefinitely.

Brooke Medicine Eagle, Native American writer on women's health issues, has spoken at length on the meaning of menopause. She speculates that perhaps hysterectomy is an opportunity for certain women to assume mature leadership roles traditionally held by their elders. Due to our longstanding deficit in women's wisdom, she sees the urgent need for its resurgence as necessitating input from younger women (albeit by the extreme of surgery). Menopause, whenever it occurs, marks a time when precious menstrual fluid, "wise blood," is retained for heightened awareness, and greater social authority. Postmenopausal women of the Grandmother Lodge are thus accorded the deepest respect and the highest honor.[13]

CELEBRATING "THE CHANGE"

In Native American and many other indigenous cultures, women at menopause are acknowledged by rituals that help them make their transition more gracefully and completely. As was mentioned earlier, menopause in our culture is often accompanied by not a little grief. What sort of ritual might we employ to help us acknowledge this sense of loss while at the same time exploring the great potential of this transition?

Most menopausal rituals naturally incorporate some way of letting go of the past and welcoming new responsibilities. Here are a few examples. The first ritual has women gather around a fire (or a symbolic candle) and take turns, one by one, giving up some fear, grief, or self-limiting belief to be consumed b . .1

vision.

In essence, the transition to cronehood signifies a time when women transmute their personal pursuits and the inherent demands of childbearing to become "keepers of the law." Their role shifts from nurturing their immediate families to caring for humanity, bringing to bear on society at large their seasoned sense of justice and harmony. The word crone is, in fact, similar in derivation to crown, signifying leadership. Even the word hag, which has such derogatory meaning in our culture, comes from the Greek "hagia," meaning "a holy one."

In this respect, it's best to have women of all ages present at a menopause celebration: crones, mothers, and maidens. In one ritual, everyone gathers around a large bowl or pot of water. Each has a cup, and each takes a turn to dip and drink, saying "I accept the wisdom of ages past." Then the crones form an inner circle, and one by one each says what she has learned in life and names the wisdom she still needs or the things she must do to complete her life's mission. As she finishes speaking, another crone dips water and gives it to her to sip, saying, "Take from the wisdom of the ages the means to fulfill your destiny." Or, "Shed the skin that has become too tight for you and be born anew."

When the crones are done, each of the other women may ask for whatever she needs to grow and be wise. As each one finishes, the elder woman to whom she is speaking gives her water to sip and repeats the blessing given above.

Although these rituals work best in groups, the same acts of letting go, naming accomplishments, and identifying the keys to one's destiny can be done in solitude. Use a candle, the water, or both, and be sure to voice your thoughts: the power of the spoken word is great. If menopausal symptoms ebb and flow over a period of years, it may be necessary to do this ritual a number of times.

SEX IN LATER YEARS

Just how satisfying and wonderful a woman's sex life will be once she is past menopause depends largely on how well she retains her self-respect and enthusiasm for living. Against all the odds, she must define herself, her continued growth, and newfound authority as valuable, despite society's views to the contrary. So pervasive is the image of older women as used-up "biddies" that this task can be difficult indeed. As our culture defines women primarily by physical beauty and ability to serve others, it's no wonder many suffer as they age, their children leave home, and family obligations lessen.

One of our finest references for tracking demeaning attitudes toward older women is Barbara Walker's *The Crone*. Walker shows that in pre-Christian culture throughout the world, the mythic triumvirate of virgin, mother, and crone reigned supreme. Christianity virtually annihilated the latter figure, retaining only the more benign and readily controlled maiden and mother.

What made the crone so threatening? In the Hindu tradition, she was known as Kali the Destroyer—not that she was maliciously violent or spiteful, but she did possess a natural instinct to terminate anything that had exhausted its usefulness in order that it might be transformed to something new. Accordingly, her power was tremendous. In myth after myth, the crone persona proved stronger than any god. As the Teutonic Elli, she conquered Thor, the god of strength. As Celtic Morgan Le Fay (or Morgan the Fate), she had the power to humble and tame all men. As Atropos the Cutter (Greek), she snipped the thread of every life.

The aspect of the crone most frightening to men is her power to reject, to refuse to care for their personal concerns, and to care instead for society at large or for fundamental principles of justice and evolution. Women's power to say no, and to see and ...

Fortunately, at least some contemporary cultures hold elder women in great esteem. In Japan, a woman reaches the highest and most venerated stage of maturity at age 61, an event marked by ceremony. In some North and South American Indian cultures, postmenopausal women acquire special status and privileges in the community as they transcend menstrual taboos. In China too, elder woman are venerated and accorded the highest respect.

But beyond honor and veneration, elder women in early ma-triarchal cultures of the Middle East and Egypt had opportunities to perform society's most important and challenging roles. They served as doctors, midwives, surgeons, health care advisors, authorities on child rearing and sexuality. As scribes, they recorded for both temple and court, maintained vital records and histories, set up calendars and official tables of weights and measures, tran-scribed and edited scriptures, and ran libraries. They were generally busier in later years than they were during the childbearing cycle. Mythology reminds us that important inventions in the fields of medicine, nutrition, and food preparation were made by women in their "years of wisdom."[15]

Besides earthly responsibilities, elder women had metaphysi-cal charges too. They took care of most religious rites and official ceremonies, from birth to death. In terms of the afterlife, it was generally believed that one was taken up in the arms of the Mother, rather than, as by Christian tenets, to the bosom of the Father. In Buddhist and other Tantric traditions, three classes of priestess—yogini, matri, and dakini—represented the virgin, mother, and crone. Dakini (the crone) literally means skywalker; devoted to the destructive aspect, she prepared the dying for death, worked with bereaved families, and administered last rites. She also knew the way into the spirit realm, and could be either fierce or gentle, depending on the dying one's behavior in life and lessons still to be learned in crossing over.

Similarly, Luisa Francia calls the crone the "goddess of the crossroads" who can hinder or block one's way, kill or allow one to pass. Stories and tales from all over the world show that the path to knowledge or true love inevitably leads through the old woman, the witch, or the woodsman. She may appear to be fragile or foolish so that no one takes her seriously, then suddenly she shows her power. In Syria, the crone was portrayed as the huge-eyed goddess Mari, who searched men's souls. The Christian adaptation of this was found in the figure of Aynat, the all-seeing Evil Eye. To a large extent, the ability to look through the veil that hid the future was the province of the crone, although superstition readily led to her being blamed for events she had merely foretold.

Yet another mythic figure symbolizing the power of the crone is Shakti, an amalgam of queenly strength, intelligence, grace, and sexuality. (Shakti, in fact, translates directly to the word vulva.) Across the board, crone figures possess a strong sexual dimension, which clearly fits with what we know of the postmenopausal increase in androgens. It's not the sensuality of the crone that is frightening to men, but the combination of sexual power with emotional and intellectual discernment.

Authors Rhonda L. Winn and Niles Newton have compiled some fascinating research about sexuality and aging. In most indigenous societies, older women were found to be extremely interested in sex. In 22 percent of those surveyed, women became markedly less inhibited with regard to sexual conversation, sexual humor, and sexual gestures as they aged. Seventy percent of societies analyzed by the authors, such as the Loredu of South Africa, the Woges of New Guinea, and the Trobriand and Eastern Islanders, showed older women having much younger men as sexual partners. Even very old women, described by observers as "toothless and decrepit," were able to obtain young and attractive boys as lovers. Often, older women played the role of sexual initiator an instructor.

Many of

...that in those societies in which sexual activity is inhibited in the aged, younger individuals tend to view the old as undesirable, or even repulsive.[16]

This has been more or less the case in the United States. According to the Consumers' Union survey in 1984 entitled *Love, Sex and Aging*, some 4,296 respondents agreed that society saw them as nonsexual. Only 65 percent of women over 70 were sexually active. Of course, we have the phenomenon of women outliving their husbands and struggling awkwardly to find new partners, overshadowed by the fear of sexually transmitted diseases. But as the baby boomer generation ages, their characteristic pursuit of self-realization will most likely extend to enduring sexual expression. And as for women outliving men, the authors of *Life Trends* predict that we will see increasing acceptance of lesbian coupling as a lifestyle option for older women (not to mention women in general).[17]

On the other hand, the longer we live, the more we as couples will spend an unprecedented number of years together. Rosalie Gilford, sociologist, sums it up this way: "Never in history have the lives of husbands and wives remained interwoven in intact marriages so long as to encounter the constellation of life-changing events that the last stages of the marital career now bring." Unsettling discoveries of differences may arise for couples in these circumstances, particularly if their lives have been organized around child rearing. This is, of course, compounded by hormonally induced role reversal. But if a couple is able to embrace these changes by having the woman take more initiative while her partner assumes a more receptive role, a natural and practical sort of androgyny may ensue.

In bed, interesting possibilities arise. The combination of men's slower arousal times and women's increased aggressiveness can lead to long, drawn-out, even ritualistic lovemaking, with women in the lead. As Charlotte reports:

> James and I have been together for 43 years. We have four grown children and seven grandchildren. I suppose our sex life in the early years was like most others: James came quickly, was a little lacking in touch and timing, and my orgasms were sporadic, at best. But I always loved to masturbate, and now, with the standards changing as they are, I find I can talk to him about the intimate details of my body. At first, I think I talked to help cover his embarrassment at slowing down, complimenting him and teaching him at the same time, you might say. But oh, the times we have now! Why, it's hours of pleasure for both of us!

Angelina has a different sort of story:

> After I went through "the change" I felt so different! Drier, sometimes, and quite unsure of myself. But I wasn't the only one! Robert took longer to come around, and wanted to spend more time touching than ever before. At first, we were rather confused by all this, but eventually, our affection and companionship deepened, and we felt more alike, more in harmony with one another.

And from Jeanne:

I'm almost 70 now, but I can't say that I feel old. Oh, sometimes I have days when I take it a bit slower, but I generally feel vigorous and self-possessed. I've had a career, you know, and children of whom I'm exceedingly proud—grandchildren, too!

Menopause was tempestuous for me because my life was so hectic then, and frankly, my marriage suffered. But a few years after, when I was about 58, something came over me and I felt this strength

... ready access to those planes—freedom to fly, I called it. Trying to account for it, well, my life was so simple, compared to my child-rearing years, and I kept myself challenged and growing with personal pursuits. Really, this was quite the opposite of what I expected sex to be like at this time of my life!

This account ties directly back to the power and authority of the crone, and raises the final question: how can we realize the full dimensions of cronehood in our present-day society? Or, to put it in Jeanne's terminology, where do we find the freedom to fly, to traverse the realms of our awareness with ease and confidence?

One approach is to act on our natural authority at this stage, seeking out opportunities to "sit in council" and employ our wisdom. Brooke Medicine Eagle speaks of the Law of Good Relationship, whereby the grandmothers had the final say in setting right any cultural imbalance. For example, if a chief was not leading the tribe in such a way that people had food, clear water, and shelter, the grandmothers asked for someone new. Or if in times of war, a chief instigated such animosity that attacks disrupted the tribe's well-being, the grandmothers might redirect him or demand that he be removed. Today, women's groups rally around the issues of peace, the environment, education, and health care, and older women need to assume their natural role of leadership and let their voices be heard. Deliberately forming an elder women's group, then finding focus within it—there may be several subgroups with distinct projects—is another possibility. In this vein, Kitzinger describes postmenopausal women in peasant societies of China and Spain, for example, as "political dynamos, wheeling and dealing, plotting and scheming."[18]

There is, however, a twist on the matter of responsibility, tied to the psychological implications of loss. Loss of youth, loss of children (once out of the home), loss of one's own parents, and ultimately, loss of interest in maintaining "the nest," may lead older women to weed out their possessions and pare down life to the essentials. Although psychiatrists may categorize these acts as symptoms of "postmenopausal depression," such nest-destroying behavior is actually quite normal. Finding the courage and vision to walk away from former entanglements or seek a simpler way of living can enable a woman to establish a new and necessary equilibrium.

Thus, in keeping with the idea of role reversal at menopause, a woman who has played an active role in the world might even choose to go into retreat, finding balance in spiritual pursuits and perhaps in solitude. Whatever we choose, the need for radical departure from obligatory roles as a means of expressing one's inner authority is key. And it is in this framework that sexual fulfillment will be realized.

1. Robert A. Wilson, *Feminine Forever* (New York: Pocket Books, 1971).

2. David Reuben, *Everything You Always Wanted to Know About Sex but Were Afraid to Ask* (New York: Bantam Books, 1971).

3. Sheila Kitzinger, *Woman's Experience of Sex* (New York: Penguin Books, 1985)

4. Susan Lark, *The Menopause Self-Help Book* (Berkeley, Calif.: Celestial Arts, 1992).

5. "Menopause: Baby Boomers' Next Step," *The Los Angeles Times* (Dec. 1989).

6. Rosetta Reitz, *Menopause: A Positive Approach* (New York: Penguin Books, 1979).

7. Susun Weed, *Menopausal Years: The Wise Woman Way* (Portland.

.... Sharpe, *Hormones: The Woman's Answer Book* (New York: Ballantine, 1987).

12. Kitzinger, *Women's Experience of Sex*.

13. Dena Taylor, *Red Flower: Rethinking Menstruation* (Freedom, Calif.: Crossing Press, 1988).

14. Barbara Walker, *The Crone* (San Francisco: Harper and Row, 1985).

15. Barbara Ehrenreich and Deirdre English, *Witches, Midwives and Nurses: A History of Women Healers* (New York: Feminist Press, 1973).

16. Rhonda L. Winn and Niles Newton, "Sexuality in Aging: A Study of 106 Cultures," *Archives of Sexual Behavior*, vol. 2, no. 4 (1982).

17. Jerry Gerber; Janet Wolff, Walter Klores, and Gene Brown, *Life Trends* (New York: Avon Books, 1989).

18. Kitzinger, *Women's Experience of Sex*.

Susan Brooks

7

Sexual Dysfunction

.... today have passed through some phase of sexual dysfunction. Of course, it all depends on how we define this. I think sexual dysfunction occurs when we have lost the ability to be sexually self-determined and have more or less sexual activity than suits us, whether by denial, inhibition, or compulsion. For example, we may overindulge in sex as an addiction, or may find ourselves unable to relate sexually due to unresolved trauma or abuse in our relationships.

We touched only briefly on abuse issues in Chapter 3, as regards pregnancy's potential to trigger recognition and acknowledgment of injuries long forgotten. In fact, it seems that abuse of women is so widespread that the real object is to be able to remember, to dredge from the depths what lies buried. How do we remember abuse?

Workshops on the subject are increasingly available, turning up on seemingly unrelated conference agendas and community college calendars. Women often attend out of curiosity, feeling somewhat bewildered as to why they are there, but by the session's end may find they recall some incident long repressed. There is a growing climate of acceptance as regards the significance of abuse on a woman's sexuality and self-esteem, her ability to mother and to form and sustain healthy relationships. Women are at last being encouraged to acknowledge this sort of experience rather than minimize it, as was previously expected.

SEX AND PHYSICAL ABUSE

There can be little doubt as to cultural attitudes surrounding abuse. Our criminal justice system has shown great reluctance to prosecute abusers, particularly on the basis of children's testimony. That females are somehow responsible for their own abuse is deeply ingrained all around the world. Women's bodies have been categorically presented as sinful and unclean, thus women are veiled, mutilated by clitorectomy, and sold millions of pounds worth of feminine hygiene sprays, deodorized pantyliners, and so on. Jurors may still believe that if a girl over the age of seven or so is abused, it is partially because she has behaved seductively, albeit unintentionally. When women are raped, they must face similar assumptions that they may be at least partially to blame. Women are grilled as to what they wore or how they behaved when the crime occurred, as though capable of playing accessory roles.

Rape is an ugly and difficult issue. One thing is clear: rape happens, and often—once every six minutes in the United States, once every ninety seconds in South Africa. Women need to take measures to protect themselves. They need to be realistic about their vulnerability and avoid situations that might jeopardize their well-being, until the world is a safer place for women in general. In the end, even if a rape case goes to trial and a woman is vindicated, she nevertheless bears scars of her violation that demand deep healing and retribution. She experiences a significant loss of herself, and must spend much time and energy making up for it.

Women who have been violently accosted and raped by a stranger cannot get the memory out of their minds. But when a woman is raped either by someone she is dating or her own husband or partner, it is somewhat easier to forget, to repress. One way to check into this for yourself is to answer the following questions. Have you ever been forced to have sex against your will? Have you ever been forcibly restrained or held down for sex while clearly indicating you wanted to be free? If so, you have indeed been raped.

The questions to unearth sexual abuse by an acquaintance or relative are more subtle and numerous. Have you ever been tricked into an intimate situation you did not desire? Has anyone ever touched you intimately against your will? Do you have a lot of trouble surrendering during intercourse? Do you hate being touched? Do you have trouble setting bound

. . . by stressful situ-
ations. Pregnancy is one example, as intense hormonal changes and complex social factors tend deeply to affect emotions. Other catalysts may include bitter arguments with loved ones, death or injury to a loved one, injury to oneself, and (yes, you guessed it) sexual activity. In short, anything that causes us to feel pushed to our limits and vulnerable is apt to release the subconscious and bring unpleasant memories to the surface.

This woman's story serves to illustrate:

We were making love and were hot into it—my husband pushed me over on my side to enter me from behind, which I really didn't want when suddenly, something just went off inside me and I panicked. Not in my head but in my heart, my gut, there was this constriction, this fear. I knew it had nothing to do with him, but I couldn't deny the feeling. Actually, I had noticed this before in other situations with men when I felt them manipulating me. I noticed the same fear and this feeling of terror, just below the surface. Part of me would freeze up and go limp, as if in survival mode.

Finally, through hypnosis, I remembered some friend of my uncle forcing me to let him play with my nipples, show him my backside and let him finger me, just a little on the outside. That's all that ever happened, but I responded in that same way back then—I froze, stood still, felt very much in danger but powerless to cry out. I felt totally humiliated, like I was no good, dirty, and it was all my fault.

Once I got over this, I could see what was happening with my husband. Whenever he was forceful with me, even if it was really okay, I just froze up—I couldn't help it. And if I let him go ahead anyway, I had those same feelings of self-loathing. We had some stuff to work out, I can tell you!

We will look more at how abuse affects sexuality in a moment. But first, here are some additional characteristics and modes of behavior common in women who have been abused that may trigger associations.

+ Describes self as never having been a child

+ Extremely concerned with control

+ Overly willing to expose genitals to others

+ Unexplained pain with intercourse

+ Extreme ideas about sexuality

+ Hypersensitive to touch

+ Repeatedly exploited by others in relationship

+ Deeply estranged from family

+ General feeling of being "under it"

+ Detaches from self and others

+ Nothing ever wrong with life, always neutral

+ Childlike behavior, dress, or appearance

+ Unkempt personal appearance

+ Chaotic surroundings and habits

+ Overly controlled surroundings or habits

+ No personal boundaries

+ No trust

+ Anger inappropriate or out of proportion to the situation

+ Inability to appreciate others

..... this list alone, it is pretty easy to extrapolate sexual-response patterns. Women who have suffered abuse show a full range of sexual behavior, from total frigidity to compulsive sexual activity and display. The latter may seem a bit surprising, but it's almost as if the victim is saying, "See, I'm so sexual and out there with it that no one can take control of me—I'm in charge." This attitude generally precludes the surrender that leads to orgasm; it almost certainly precludes intimacy. Actually, this is the quintessentially masculine approach of using sex primarily for self-gratification, without placing it in the context of a relationship. Women who have been abused may unconsciously reject their feminine vulnerability to be more on a par with their oppressor. Clarrise related, "In retrospect, it's like I bought into the beliefs of the man who abused me. My cunt was just a cunt, and I used it that way, keeping myself separate from it, using it as much as I could to prove the point that it was not me, I didn't have to be connected."

It is easy to correlate discomfort with touch or intercourse to sexual abuse, but the psychological damage that leads to increased vulnerability to disease, accidents, and career instability is more complex. Many characteristics of abusees are in fact contradictory,

though notably extreme. The manic-depressive personality often
correlates to a history of sexual abuse.

Besides the obvious means of physical or sexual abuse, there
are many other ways or instances in which women may feel
abused. How many of us, for example, have felt violated during a
gynecological examination, as procedures were done or tools used
forcibly to examine us when we clearly were not ready? Or perhaps we have felt patronized after the examination, as our intimate questions and concerns were brushed aside or ridiculed.
Women often report feeling abused by birthing procedures that
involve overuse of technology or invasion of privacy. These sorts of
abuse, less clear-cut because so widespread and culturally acceptable, nevertheless affect women in characteristic fashion: self-esteem and self-worth are diminished, personal boundaries are lost or
disrupted, and sexual response and satisfaction are likely to be
altered.

In my many years of practicing women's health, I have had
ample experience with women suffering from what is commonly
known as vaginism, or vaginismus: an uncontrollable contraction
of the vaginal muscles whenever penetration is attempted. This is
especially sad to see in very young women, particularly if the cause
is that their first gynecological examination was so rough that they
now find it difficult to have intercourse, let alone regular check-
ups. Of course, vaginismus is also a classic sign of sexual abuse.

When working with a woman who has this problem, I go out
of my way to put her in control. I use a very small speculum, for
example, and have her insert it herself. Sometimes this is not
possible, and we need to start from the most basic point of having
her put her finger inside to find the involuntary contraction response so she can work directly on relaxing the muscles. Of course
this takes time, but her sense of mastery as she begins to overcome
her fear makes it completely worthwhile. This alone will not cure
her condition; she may find that the same involuntary response
occurs the next time she tries to have intercourse. But at least she
may feel confident enough to communicate with her partner and
discuss her needs and her fears.

If she cannot come to terms with her situation, she may find it possible to have sex only by detaching herself. She may enjoy clitoral stimulation and orgasm but, feeling herself close as she is entered, will then pull back in silence and shame. This is tragic because the pattern perpetuates itself, and the woman remains a victim.

Classic therapeutic techniques for vaginismus include behavioral approaches of reimprinting. A

.... approaches is that they may not allow her the necessary release of emotion, particularly of anger. Besides, penetration is not the be-all and end-all of sexual pleasure for women that it is for men. Penetration affords very little stimulation to the clitoris; thus it follows that women do not necessarily need penetration to find sexual fulfillment.

The best approach for a woman struggling with vaginismus is to talk with her partner and reach an exploration agreement. That is, the two of them agree to let her take the lead in showing him all the finer points of what is arousing to her—her particulars of pleasure. She can first show him exactly what she does when she masturbates, where and how she likes to be touched. Then she can guide him to try the same—only that, and no more.

Sheila Kitzinger has described this technique step-by-step and recommends that from this point, penetration occur only with the woman's own finger as mutual pleasuring continues. The woman's partner can climax outside her, in her hand or between her legs, wherever feels okay with her. Above all, both she and her partner should agree in advance that she will be free to stop the process at any time. Eventually, it may be his finger inside her or his penis, but she must always be in control and in charge of the pace, doing as much as or as little as seems right to her each time.

Some women find they actually prefer sex without penetration, and the couple then needs to work out some mutually acceptable arrangement.

In a similar vein are the traumas attendant to delivering a baby with an unplanned or undesired episiotomy. As discussed in Chapter 4, there are certain practical considerations in healing the vaginal area when there has been injury or trauma, and most women who have had repair have a certain amount of hesitation the first time they have sex. But some feel more than hesitation. The psychological trauma of episiotomy may link to a feeling of violation. Women speak of being mutilated, changed, no longer themselves. The net result is similar to that of sexual abuse: the sufferer feels shame, guilt, and inadequacy for having been con- taminated or affected, as if it were all her fault.

Working through a negative cycle of sexual identification requires, in most cases, an opportunity to relive the key event in vivid and clear detail. This should trigger the original reaction, which may then be transformed into something more self-affirm- ing. Unfortunately, many women never have an opportunity to get past their anger. Finding so little external validation for what they feel, they direct their fury and frustration at themselves, in self-im- molation. The healing process must also incorporate an objective look at the situation. With episiotomy, for example, documenta- tion is readily available on its exorbitant overuse in the United States as opposed to European countries, not to mention the lack of practitioner training here in skills to maintain an intact per- ineum. A woman needs to share with her partner her fear, shame, anger, and her need for both reassurance and enough autonomy to find her own way to heal. If there is anything we health workers ought to know by now, it's that whatever happens to a woman's body also happens to her spirit. She may temporarily separate these so that they may better reunite, but she cannot (and must never be expected to) divorce the two.

EMOTIONAL ABUSE

Emotional abuse is certainly a component of physical abuse. When a woman is raped, she suffers much more than physical injury; the comments and insults of her attacker have as far-reaching effects as the degradation of her body. Girls who are victims of incest feel the psychological manipulation to be just as devastating as the physical violation.

But ~~~~~~~~~~~~~~

, - ~~~~~~, trace vulnerability back to early childhood experience, particularly with regard to bonding and attachment. According to Avodah Offit, M.D., author of *The Sexual Self*, sexual behavior is very much influenced by the degree to which we have bonded to another in infancy, which in turn affects how well we deal with the anxiety of separation. As stated earlier, if we are kept close and secure when small, we become more comfortable with ourselves and better able to tolerate being alone. If, as claimed by William James, "The greatest terror of infancy is solitude," perhaps we need to reexamine the manner in which we gain independence. In an era of putting our children on their own at an early age, it's time we saw these patterns of parenting behavior for what they are: survival strategies and adaptations in a culture moving way too fast for intimate relationships. We will not find the strength to save our planet, save our souls, or experience sexual ecstasy by isolation! Our need to attach to others, to depend on them, is perfectly normal and healthy. We remember the touch and security (hopefully) of our mother's body, which we naturally seek again with another.

A great turning point and reckoning in this regard occurs when we first fall in love. Separation anxiety becomes intense as we realize that in bonding and attaching so deeply to another, our bonds to our parents will be forever changed. Our needs to be close, to be protected and to protect, are suddenly transferred to someone new.

Ideally, separation anxiety and the desire for closeness that it engenders will motivate us to endure the challenging stages of intimate relationship: marriage, childbearing and rearing, illness and death. It might well be said that strong mother/infant attachment is really the basis of our ability to meet life's onslaughts with courage and equanimity. If this initial attachment is hindered, whether by social, economic, or physiological disruptions, things may predictably go awry. Our subsequent attachments are likely to be inhibited or fractional. The more our ability to relate to others is impaired, the greater our anxiety and dependence. And it is thus that we become targets for emotional abuse.

Even if our original attachments are sound, so vulnerable are we at the time of first love that a whole new configuration of imprints may occur. In his book *Restoring Innocence*, Alfred Ellis suggests that we can often trace unsatisfying and dysfunctional relationship patterns to our experience of first love. The following questions might serve to illuminate this for you. Did your first love share his/her heart with you or just his/her body? Was he/she patient and kind, or inconsiderate? Was he/she honest and forthright with you, or deceiving and untrue? Did the relationship end amicably or with unresolved anger, pain, and humiliation? Did you feel in any way abused by him/her?

This brings us back to the beginning: what, exactly, is emotional abuse? It is any behavior designed to control or subjugate another through emotionally based techniques of intimidation, ridicule, invalidation, manipulation, or verbal assault? Sometimes it's easier to recognize the effects of emotional abuse than the behavior, particularly for women who have practically become used to being abused. If you are suffering from low self-esteem, lack of trust in your perceptions, inability to appreciate your accomplishments, lack of motivation, chronic depression, or difficulty in taking charge of your life, you may be a victim.

In *The Emotionally Abused Woman*, Beverly Engel gives us several typical profiles of abuses. Each of these, she notes, finds a complement in a particular type of abuser. Abusers can be anyone in a role of authority: parents, teachers, bosses, mentors, or religious leaders. Or they may be peer counterparts such as siblings, lovers, friends, or coworkers.

Interestingly enough, Engel's profiles correspond closely with those women found by Offit to be most prone to

.... an experi-

.... of powerlessness, self-abnegation, or denigration. Frequently, we find ourselves in one pattern or another just as we begin to care deeply for someone; it is precisely at this point that our most basic emotions and fundamental responses are touched and triggered.

Here, then, are five profiles of abusees, composite of Engel's and Offit's observations combined with my own. There are strong similarities among the first four, but crucial differences in the sort of partner each type of woman tends to select.

Selfless and Silent

This woman has usually been dominated, controlled, or neglected in her young years to such an extreme degree that she has little or no sense of self. She may take on the personality of others, particularly when in love—anything to be accepted. On the other hand, intimacy is both frightening and threatening to her.

When it comes to sex, women in this pattern move in and out of relationships with great frequency. Sex may be either deeply inhibited and unsatisfying or explosive, releasing deep and overwhelming emotions that cannot be integrated. Women stuck in this role are in a turmoil when in love, empty when not. As one of my clients confided to me: "I don't really know how to be close to a man, but I sure do try. Usually I try to be like him, doing what he likes to do—even in bed, no matter what. Sometimes I feel hurt, sometimes used and very sad, and sometimes this fury rises up in me and I have to get away. I hate that though, because when I'm by myself I don't know who I am. That scares me so much I start looking for someone else right away."

With this kind of fearful overlay, intimacy of any kind is virtually impossible. As Offit observes, "In bed, dependence more often leads to erotic extinction than to an eternal flame of passion."[3] Women of the silent/selfless temperament are usually attracted to their opposite, highly self-involved types who have little or no ability to care for another. The longer a woman stays with a partner like this, the more she will be drawn into his or her narcissistic, grandiose schemes. If and when she decides to leave, she will have to cope with the loss of all she has invested, plus a further diminished sense of self.

Women thus afflicted need serious help through hypnosis, long-term psychotherapy or other deep work in order to trace patterns of self-abuse back to their original source. It is doubtful that women caught in this role would even read a book such as this, but if you have a loved one you are trying to help, encourage her to seek professional assistance.

Servile and Compulsive

This role is also excessively dependent, centering around the expectations of others. Almost every woman in today's world has some "pleaser" in her, so deeply ingrained is the expectation that women should put others' needs before their own. If taken to an extreme, this type will tolerate and suffer the demeaning and abusive behavior of others to an extent that is utterly damaging to all concerned. Just as she blames herself for the misdeeds of her intimates, she likewise impedes them from taking responsibility for their own actions. If she happens to have a moment of clarity and notices how others take advantage of her, she will likely slip into apology for her own behavior, fully repressing herself and remaining dependent.

Why does a woman behave thus? Often, her parents demanded perfection and routinely ignored her personal boundaries and limitations. She may have been berated simply for being female (perhaps a son was sorely desired). Whatever the cause, this is a woman unlikely to find happiness in bed. She is far too busy evaluating her performance, assessing it by her partner's standards. "Was it good enough?" she wonders.

...ce, and so ..., ...aid of losing control, of letting the ...ster of her own frustrated needs and desires out of the bag.

Characteristically, she does not reach orgasm with intercourse. It goes without saying, I hope, that there are many other reasons for anorgasmia, but as part of the syndrome, a woman in this pattern cannot acknowledge herself fully enough to let go. For her, the "petite mort" of orgasm is downright terrifying. As Karen related, "I try to give my lover everything she wants in bed—I give and give until frankly, I feel weak and sick inside. Nothing I do seems to really excite her, and when she finally comes, I start worrying about what she's thinking and whether or not I pleased her. I know I shouldn't say this, but I'd rather put my energy into the house or my work, where I know I can do some good."

Ironically, this woman is often paired with a controlling type, one who continually reinforces her need to please by being hyper-critical.

The servile/compulsive women needs to see that life is not about meeting some outside standard of perfection; it's about personal growth and development. The key here is risk taking, in relatively comfortable but challenging situations. This means doing things strictly for personal pleasure and enrichment: starting from scratch at singing lessons or dance, for example, or trying anything that beckons to one's inner longing. More than any other type, this woman can find happiness by contacting and healing her child self, getting back on her own track in life. Sexually, she needs a new foundation based upon her own needs and desires. And she may need a counselor's help in identifying the best place to start.

Guilt-Ridden and Reactive

This role is otherwise known as that of the "sinner." The woman playing it is more in touch with her desires than the other types discussed thus far, but all that her passions bring her is guilt and shame. For the most part, she is so burdened with self-loathing that she can scarcely think about perfection. Women entrenched in this pattern usually have suffered severe physical as well as emotional abuse when young, believing (as they were told) that their naughtiness, seductiveness, or worthlessness was just cause for their violation. As adults, they remain in reaction to these beliefs. Engel puts it most succinctly: "Sinners believe that bad things only happen to bad people."[4]

As you might expect, these women pair up with those ready to reinforce their guilt by blaming them for everything under the sun, which only serves to perpetuate their feelings of unworthiness. Blamers are always right; sinners, always wrong. As Sharon revealed, "My boyfriend says terrible things to me sometimes, and I know I should forgive him but I just can't. Then I see even more how he's right—I really am a terrible person. I don't do the shopping on time because I want to read, or I forget to pay bills because I'm out with my friends." What about her sex life? "I'm pretty scared and nervous about sex—I always mess it up. Sometimes I cry and have to stop, I feel so awful inside, and he tells me it's all my fault. He's right, of course, but that just makes it worse. The truth is, I like sex, but I hate what it does to me."

Reactive women literally absorb their partner's ills and delusions, being sponge-like and compliant. So utterly out of balance do their primary relationships become that often they refer to life and love as nothing but pain—a natural result, really, of such gross disharmony and oppression. Often, there's a history of alcoholism or drug abuse in the family. Again, deep work to get to the roots of self-deprecation is in order.

Passive and Victimized

Women playing a passive role are targets for victimization and tragedy. ~~Sexually~~ ~~~~ ~~1~~

~~partners are~~ in the explosively danger-ous position of having full sway, often to the point of extreme verbal or physical abuse. The victim tells herself she deserves it, that she's inept or just plain crazy. Frequently she has witnessed a similar pattern at home between her father and mother.

Sometimes this woman's partner is something of a sexual so-ciopath: one who lives for sexual conquest. Offit notes that the sociopath is admired and loved by all—except his (or her) inti-mates. He deviously and methodically manipulates his partner into submission by never responding to her advances but insisting she respond to his, or by giving her affection only when she is ex-tremely busy so he can then accuse her of not being spontaneous. He may even lead her to question her sanity by pretending never to have said or done things he in fact said or did quite deliberately. He is a master at making others feel uncomfortable while seeming to do nothing at all.[5]

Sex is likely to run just one way: he is always in charge, calling the shots. She will be made to feel ignorant, incomplete, inadequate, and may come to believe that there is something seri-ously wrong with her body, her technique. As Julie says, "The only time sex was any good for me was when we were making up—it gave me a chance to express my love to Gene, to reassure myself that he still loved me. The rest of the time I felt too insecure to make any moves in bed, and I don't think Gene wanted me to anyway—I had so many problems. Sometimes, though, I let him force me into it. I suffered through, hoping I could improve myself in his eyes."

These are the women who report that their partners, "wonderful men," have told them that their vaginas are too loose, tight, long or short, their orgasms not strong enough, their intensity not quite up to par, their nipples not hard enough, and so on, and so on. Amazingly, many of these victims are otherwise competent women who either lack experience with sex or have never been particularly in touch with their bodies. Not knowing about themselves makes it easy for them to believe they are deficient, particularly in a culture with role models such as ours.

Passive victims can often be helped by contact with support groups, aided by articulating deep-seated insecurities and feelings of anxiety while overcoming their isolation. Working with women's health, I am saddened by the frequency with which women question the adequacy of their bodies and the appearance of breasts and genitals that are perfectly normal. I find myself time and again telling women during breast examinations that regardless of size, the breasts usually flop apart when a woman lies down, despite cultural premiums on "stand-up tits." Sometimes a woman will point to her labia and ask if the size, color, or general appearance is okay. It is important to remember that sexist conditioning victimizes us as surely as more direct forms of abuse.

Hysterical and Overdrawn

This is the last type we will consider. The word hysterical actually derives from the Latin word for uterus, and common use of the term reflects back to a time when it was believed that an irrational or excitable woman was under the influence of uterine "ethers" moving about her body. Of late, the term histrionic has come into favor as being less derogatory. I rather like hysterical because it implies a woman under the influence of feminine energies and forces, albeit to an extreme.

At any rate, women thus oriented thrive on intensity, high drama, and chaos. Very often, their lives when young were either strictly controlled and inhibited or filled with crisis and disruption. Either way, these women feel most alive and comfortable in the midst of (or while making) a scene. They seek out situations that engender strong emotions like anger or jealousy—anything to ...

or drug abuser, compulsive gambler, sex addict, or one in trouble with the law. Or she may select the "hard cases," individuals so disturbed that they are nearly impossible to reach. She may also go for someone unavailable (married, for example) or clearly not interested. She is *not* apt to meet a healthy, somewhat normal person with a decent likelihood of loving her and treating her respectfully.

Ultimately, this woman uses drama as a smoke screen to avoid looking at her own problems and to keep them from getting her attention. Of course, her partner is doing the same; it is the main thing they have in common. The difference is that for the histrionic woman, tension is her drug, and she uses it to keep chaos at a level that feels comfortable. Setting ultimatums, staging rescues, arguments, and the like, she literally takes on her partner's problems as her own, creating so much stress in the relationship that abuse may come as a welcome release.

Sexually, it's a roller coaster. This woman's counterpart often has a highly changeable and erratic personality (Dr. Jekyll/Mr. Hyde, according to Engel) which will of course be intensified by drugs, alcohol, or criminal intrigue. Sex can be unbelievably hot and explosive, but at the same time riddled with cruelty and manipulation. The most noticeably absent quality in both partners is genuine vulnerability.

Here's a typical report: "The best thing about our relationship was the sex. I loved trying to entice Jack into sex when he wasn't really in the mood. Sometimes I'd have to make a scene, accuse and argue with him just to get him angry and really hot for me. Then he'd take me to the limit, and I'd scream and holler my way to oblivion. Other times he was cold, cruel, and calculating. If I let him make love to me like that, he would trick me out—you know, make it hard for me to come, or make me come at the wrong time. I'd be so angry, I'd pull way back. Then he would apologize, and we'd have blowout sex again."

Note the contradictions here: on the one hand, sex was "the best thing," on the other hand, it was degrading. Clearly, this woman must identify her real need, that of stability and security within herself. Until she can wean herself off the exhilaration that comes from constant crisis, she will be destined for a life of burnout. She must learn to use her need for excitement in constructive ways. Even though not drug- or alcohol-dependent herself, she may benefit from contact with an abusers' or a family of alcoholics' group, exploring the characteristics of relationship under the shadow of dependency.

If we are truthful with ourselves, we will recognize that we have all played at least one, and probably several, of these roles at some point. Whether abuse is emotional or physical, it all comes down to the same thing: powerlessness, and the need to do something about it. Methods of recovery are many and various, ranging from long-term counseling to self-directed work on our issues. The latter may involve dealing directly or indirectly with both original and current abusers, making known all the reasons for anger and hurt, as well as a list of wants and needs from each.

Another cardinal rule: a woman should give herself full permission to do as little or as much work on these issues as feels right. Any woman who has felt forced or compelled into intimate contact against her best interests needs space, and the freedom to work always by her own inner clock. If she pushes herself at all, she will sink back into the same familiar patterns of powerlessness. Like so much else about us, work on healing is rhythmic: two steps forward, one step back, rather like delivering a baby. Acknowledging one's limitations is the key to moving beyond them.

SEXUAL ADDICTION

...en sex is a drug, used to avoid life's difficulties or to seek attention and validation that should really come from inside, then there is a problem. It's a fine line: we all use sex for reassurance and to address our most basic needs for touch and intimate contact. But when sexual activity becomes destructive of our work or professional relationships, or when it is hurtful to others, sexuality is no longer in its proper life-affirming place.

Consider this case history of a woman caught in negative and compulsive sexual behavior. Tina reported a tempestuous and stressful phase in a career she actually wanted to escape from; she was overworked and exhausted. She met up with an old friend, now married, and, despite her better judgment, started sleeping with him. In her own words:

> It's not like we were in love. I felt comfortable with him, and it was a release. But the more I did it, the less I felt. I don't know quite how to describe it; it was like I was emotionally dead inside. Still, he took care of me.
>
> Then, of all things, I got pregnant! I haven't been pregnant but once before and this was a total accident, total carelessness. It shocked me into seeing what I was doing. I

wasn't taking care of myself at all—just using sex to get by. I had an abortion and ended the relationship.

Here, an otherwise assertive and successful woman became a passive victim in an intimate relationship. The stress, the uncertainty, the inability to face the changes impending in her life led to some very self-destructive and painful behavior.

Another example from Janelle, married with a child:

My husband was the classic executive, straight-arrow, in his head all the time, tense and anxious. After our son was born, sex just stopped. I felt like I had dried up inside, that I was losing my beauty and my charm. I started an affair with a man in the neighborhood—he was unemployed and his wife worked—I even knew her slightly. He had problems, and I tried to help. It was so wonderful to be needed, to be admired, to have that hot kind of sex that is just so good! But after a while I started seeing him for what he was—a troubled man, a loser, really, and somebody else's husband. Quite suddenly I saw how I'd been using him to avoid the disappointment I felt in my own marriage and my anxieties about getting a life of my own. It was a rude awakening to things I'd been putting off for a long time.

Examples like this abound. But then, there is sexual addiction that involves the apparently insatiable appetite, bringing to mind nymphomania. Is there really such a condition per se, or is it merely a symptom of other emotional or psychological problems? Probably the latter: most sexologists see the condition as resulting from a lack of healthy attachment and separation experiences. Nymphomaniacs can't bear to be alone; they crave to a nearly manic extent the comforts of human contact, presumably to make up for some deprivation when young.

Most of us have known or heard of women like these, in bed with a new man almost every night, always "on the make." They have so much basic anxiety that intercourse, no matter how frequent, doesn't make so much as a dent in their insecurity. Some are multiorgasmic and may climax as many as 20 or more times in one sexual experience, able to stop only when totally exhausted. Others report orgasms to be unfulfilling and monotonous. The great majority are rarely orgasmic. The uncontrollable aspect of their behavior causes so much stress that it is impossible to relax and release. In short, women in this pattern are profoundly immature, very deeply injured and repressed from years before

There is another

─ ── ──

1. Laura Davis and Ellen Bass, *The Courage to Heal* (New York: Harper and Row, 1988).

2. Sheila Kitzinger, *Women's Experience of Sex* (New York: Penguin Books, 1985).

3. Avodah K. Offit, *The Sexual Self* (New York: J.B. Lippincott, 1977).

4. Beverly Engel, *The Emotionally Abused Woman* (Los Angeles: Lowell House, 1990).

5. Offit, *The Sexual Self*.

8

Sexual Abstinence

, pervades our cultural definition of happiness and fulfillment that a woman going without is automatically presumed to be deprived and longing. As will be shown in the following pages, nothing could be further from the truth, at least when abstinence is a choice.

In fact, more and more women are deciding to take time off from sexual activity when preoccupied with personal issues and problems. Social autonomy has set the stage for women's emotional self-determination. The cultural constraints of the 1950s that defined sex for women as either taboo or obligatory no longer hold sway. Women may be categorically portrayed in the media as sex objects, but they are increasingly shown to have sexual identities and lives of their own. That a woman would, under circumstances of stress or emotional strain, decide it best to keep her vital energies to herself is certainly understandable.

To illustrate, here is a story of my own experience some years ago. My husband and I were going through a particularly difficult time in our relationship; we were not yet married (a bone of contention between us) and were working out negative consequences of an affair he had had some time earlier. That these issues were disrupting our sex life was quite natural, to my thinking, although

I won't deny I was concerned. Our therapist, who had additional training in sex therapy, showed us a tape one day of a couple engaged in foreplay according to specific recommendations and step-by-step instructions. This experience both mortified and frustrated me, and I told her outright, "I don't *need* this, I don't think we have any problems with technique. My problem is with my feelings, my pain and vulnerability, the trust issue. I think if we work on these, I'll want to have sex again." This is not to minimize sex therapy for those with unusual aversions or physical difficulties, but for the vast majority of women, sexual dysfunction is emotionally based, and nothing more. We don't need another survey to tell us that a woman cannot be loving, open, and orgasmic if she feels her partner is treating her poorly or unfairly, let alone if she can't do right by herself.

What is it like to take a sexual time-out? It depends on the situation, but most women report a typical progression from loneliness to self-confidence and clarity. Brenda, a single, career-oriented woman in her thirties, tells how a series of relationships frightened her into abstinence that then became voluntary for a period of seven months.

> I had an outrageous affair with a fellow who turned out to be royalty, a Scottish lord in fact. It was a whirlwind romance— in a matter of weeks he proposed marriage. On the one hand, I knew I'd be "taken care of" for life, and all my friends were telling me to go for it. But this is a pattern that keeps reoccurring in my life—guys go crazy for me, and the situation becomes overwhelming. Maybe I have something to do with it—after all, I let it happen, to a point. Then I feel this pressure of being swept away, and I notice that it happens more when I'm unsettled or stressed at work.
>
> So, I said no to this guy with *much* relief, and then the same thing happened with a man who turned out to be married—there were signs and signals that I never followed up until it was way too late. After this I pulled back completely from men and sex.

Being celibate for all these months has given me some important things. One is protection—I can feel vulnerable with myself and not be at risk. Another is a very clear picture of what I want in relationship: marriage to the right man. Eventually, because now I'm content to wait.

Other comments from women in similar circumstances: "I'm ⸻ ⸺". "I see the seeds of myself

strual phase. In examining ⸻

these were culturally imposed by men or formulated by women themselves. Nevertheless, ritual isolation while menstruating gives women the opportunity to be celibate for a few days, to disentangle themselves from routine obligations, and to reflect on personal issues in the company of others doing the same. Perhaps we all need such a respite, a chance to have body and soul to ourselves periodically without guilt or anxiety. Without this, we may manifest patterns of self-denial and subservience.

Let us examine this premise by way of example, taking first that of Lynda, who explains:

I grew up in a household where mom's main task was taking care of everyone else's business. I loved her for it, hated her for it, learned to depend on her and not myself. Even though we fought bitterly when I was in my teens, I found myself continually dependent and wanting to please her before myself, even as an adult. Three marriages and three children later, I still don't know all that much about me. My sexuality has been restrained, I think, confined to what's expected. I've been abstinent for three months now, and it's been a good way for me to sort things out and get to the heart of who I am. To tell you the truth, I feel like a child now, discovering broken threads from the past and reweaving them. Right now, I don't want anyone else but me.

This points to a primary need of women throughout time, that of self-containment. *Women and Madness*, by Phyllis Chesler, explores the consequence of diffusing the self for the ease and pleasure of others until complete disintegration of personality threatens to occur. When a woman rallies from this position it is usually with passion and fury; a passion that requires no other partner than herself.

Sometimes sexual excess leads to celibacy. This too is a classic theme, and women are not exempt. Here is what Alena has to say:

> I was rather repressed when I was young, living in a house that was immaculately clean and bound by strict rules of behavior. There was love, but there was also fear; my mom was afraid of herself, I guess. I took the road less traveled (at least in my family) and dropped out of school. I met wild and wonderful people, and found I could make good money selling sexual favors. Not prostitution exactly, but intimate massages, blow jobs, that kind of thing. I was choosy, though, and never a slave to anyone. For a while I felt free, for the first time in my life. Then good friends turned bad, a few died of drug overdoses, and I turned to religion. I needed to purify myself, and I didn't have sex with anyone for three years.

As we enter our second decade of confronting HIV and AIDS, stories like this become increasingly rare. Nevertheless, sexual addiction and overindulgence remain major pathways to celibacy for a number of women.

More commonly, women complain of feeling prostituted in seemingly conventional relationships. Often this comes from repressing the pain of unmet needs, or of being ignored or belittled.

The result is that sex becomes quite sporadic: a few encounters over a period of a day or two (perhaps after an argument) and then weeks with no contact. Recent research has shown that sporadic ⋯⋯al activity is more likely to cause menstrual irregularity and ⋯⋯ celibacy. (Orgasm via masturbation does not ⋯⋯ular sex, or none at all, tends to

⋯ ₋ 1

⋯ ·ᵎᵉ so

My husband was un⋯⋯
years to acknowledge it. Once I ⋯⋯,
ousy and fear. I started having anxiety attacks, eve⋯ ₋
places. I'd just be going along fine, when suddenly I'd feel breathless, lightheaded; my heart would be racing and I'd have to sit down. I ended my marriage, but the same thing happened with the next guy. I finally realized that sex had become so full of fear and pain for me that I would probably keep losing again and again, unless I broke the cycle on my own. So I quit looking for validation from men, for breath-taking romance, and got down to being by myself. Some days I felt so alone that panic and anxiety nearly got me, but eventually, I could catch these feelings right away and set myself free. I discovered the things that nourished me and made me feel complete, instead of trying to fit other people's notions of what I should be.

Pain and heartbreak aside, it is time for women to recognize that the sexes definitely differ in erotic temperament. According to research presented in *Brain Sex*, there is overwhelming evidence that men are by nature polygamous and tend to focus on sex for its own sake.[2] This does not preclude romance or even monogamous commitment, but a woman needs to know what she is up against. In any case, happiness comes not from seeking some idealized version of masculinity. Accepting men for what they are is the first step toward strengthening our own position. Relationships involve conflict because male and female desires appear to be at odds, but they can also be viewed as complementary. Each sex has certain basic needs that are fairly consistent; John Gray has illuminated this quite well. For example, women need to feel cared for and loved in order to be able to trust their partners. Men, on the other hand, need to be trusted in order to give; a man without a woman's trust loses his momentum, his vitality. Naturally, men will fail to care for women as women would like, and women will find reason to lose trust in men, but that doesn't change the basic needs of each. The more realistic we are about differences between the sexes, and the more we accept our own traits and tendencies, the better we will be at weathering the ups and downs in relationships, the inevitable challenges and disappointments.

When a woman chooses sexual abstinence, she has the opportunity to own both her masculine and feminine aspects and bring them to terms with one another. For example, she can look at how much love and nourishment she gives to herself, and, if minimal, at the resulting lack of trust and vulnerability she feels with others. This will not change her basic needs once she is in a relationship: no matter how well she has learned to care for herself, she will still be vulnerable to a lack of caring from her partner. However, she may be better equipped to deal with breakdowns in communication and estrangement when they occur and go on caring for herself regardless.

How positive or constructive a period of abstinence is for a woman largely depends on how deliberate it is. When abstinence is by choice, negative side effects such as depression, lack of motivation, and disinterest in personal hygiene may not occur. Note that just as it may benefit a woman to be free of overconcern for her appearance, her self-esteem may be negatively affected if she doesn't keep herself up. More than occasional depression demands attention, and perhaps assistance. Counseling can help, as can time spent regularly with other women in group process or circle. Starting a woman's circle is not all that difficult; you can make your

time together whatever you want, perhaps with ritual and planned
discussion of topics such as money, sexuality, jealously, or whatever
feels relevant from meeting to meeting. Another possibility is to
choose a book on women's issues or ritual celebrations and work
with In my experience, great revelations can occur
professional assistance. One reason
for sexual absti-
a

we see this
from flattering, such as old
of witch burnings, it is notable that the
were single women of advanced age, so unacceptable
women to refuse to be vessels for male satisfaction and procreation.[5]

Some women worry about needing sexual contact to remain
physically youthful and attractive. Certainly masturbation can
serve to relieve tension, stimulate pelvic circulation, provide pleasure and the benefits of oxytocin. And there are innumerable ways
to find physical satisfaction and emotional and spiritual release
that have little to do with sex. Some women just don't want sex,
whatever the reason, and that's all there is to it. Ultimately,
women are more autonomous than men in this regard because they
are better able to incorporate the erotic in all aspects of life.

What, if any, are the physical effects of long-term abstinence? With so many motivating factors, it is difficult to general-
ize. Some women do notice symptoms of pelvic tension such as
chronic backache, increased premenstrual tension, or menstrual
difficulties, but just as many report cessation of the above, particularly when abstinent after ending a miserable relationship. Occasionally, women report losing touch with the monthly cycle,
becoming less aware of fertile and premenstrual signals. If fertility
awareness was used contraceptively, this is certainly understandable. But perhaps these women are merely revising emotional
and spiritual aspects of cycling to suit their newfound autonomy;

most state that abstinency clears the way for more honest acknowledgment of feelings.

Many women notice increased awareness of diet and health when on their own. Without the distraction of another's needs, they are better able to see the results of their own eating and lifestyle habits, and to experiment with what makes them feel best. Particularly if a woman has been living with someone and cooking and eating more to suit his or her wishes than her own, she may find this aspect of being alone most illuminating and beneficial.

Women often say that the less sex they have, the less they think about it. Sometimes the longing for contact is strong, but usually it is more a desire for intimacy than sex itself (unless a woman is peak-fertile or premenstrual). Being celibate is less about not having sex than it is about being alone, dealing with one's own body, psyche, and soul. The periodic desire for intimacy is part of the deal and should be seen as a personal manifestation of need rather than the result of having someone attractive around.

Other reasons why a woman might choose to avoid having sex temporarily have little to do with relationship. For example, a woman friend of mine recently shared plans for a year-long trip around the world and her decision to forego sexual involvement until she left. No dates, no serious flirting, just packing and settling affairs. Similar indications might be plans to move house, change career, or focus on a creative project. As a spiritual discipline, celibacy has long been reputed to enhance one's concentration if undertaken with clear and serious resolve: something all women should think about and keep open as an option.

And what if a woman elects to take this option in spite of the fact that she is married or in intimate partnership? We read and hear much about differences in sexual desire between partners and, at last, the periodic desire for abstinence is coming out of the closet. National surveys on the frequency of sex deal in averages only. One must figure in the less-than-desired episodes and unsatisfactory contacts, as well as the flurry of sexual activity common in the initial stages of a relationship when major challenges to intimacy have yet to be faced. I can think of no long-term study that reflects the phases of closeness and separation in enduring relationships.

How *does* a couple get by when one wants sex and the other ⌐⌐? Ideally they discuss the matter and set themselves limits. ⌐⌐ become acute, they may decide they ⌐⌐ frequently challenged ⌐⌐ of

⌐⌐.

could come from ⌐⌐.

Personal trauma of any kind is ⌐⌐. ple's sex life, particularly the loss of a loved one. The ⌐ child, a parent, or a dear friend or relative may cause either a desperate need for contact or complete disinterest. If only one partner is affected, the other may provide stable ground. But if both are devastated, as by the loss of a child, getting into the emotional intensity of sex may be just too much to handle. Rhythms of processing grief may also be at odds so that when one partner is raw and vulnerable, the other is shut down and unable to feel much of anything. Here is Amanda's story of what happened to her after the death of her son at eight weeks from crib death, or SIDS (Sudden Infant Death Syndrome):

> I don't think there is anything more horribly painful on earth than losing a child, at least, I hope there's not, because I don't think I could endure it. Jerry and I had many sad and upsetting experiences trying to make love after Jason's death, but this one time was so amazing I must share it with you. We were fucking and crying, really, fucking and crying, when we felt something descend on us, a great break in the tension, a feeling of warmth and healing. It was so wonderful, I can't tell you—a perfect state of grace. Sex aside, orgasms aside, in that moment, time stood still and we felt whole

again. After this, we stopped doubting and blaming ourselves so much. The guilt began to lift, and we began to live life again.

Reestablishing intimacy after any kind of intensely painful experience or shock is a difficult process; this couple was lucky to find common ground. Time heals, more than anything else. Realigning oneself after deep trauma is hardly a simple matter; layer upon layer must be permeated with new hope, definition, and resolve. For a time, we strongly encouraged people to express their grief profoundly and immediately; we now see that mourning and grieving are in fact cyclic processes and may take years and years to complete. The same is true, by the way, for anyone recovering from experiences of physical, emotional, or sexual abuse. Tina relates: "Pat and I had known each other for about a year, while she was still living with her previous partner. Then she and I became intimate, and she decided to leave Sue. She felt great guilt about this decision, along with new sadness and confusion regarding patterns of passivity from childhood abuse. Just as she became free to be with me, she decided she couldn't be sexual for a while. That was okay; I understood." Coping with the effects of debilitating illness, handicap, or mutilating surgery such as mastectomy or hysterectomy may also call for a sexual time off.

Sometimes the desire for abstinence becomes permanent, as in Joan's case:

I'm 69 now, and my husband died six years ago. A couple of years after his death, friends tried to set me up with men, and at first I was curious, interested. But each time it was so obviously wrong that all I felt was revulsion. I'd think to myself, "I have to get in bed with *that?*" I had such a wonderful marriage, and now I have my children and grandchildren. I've got used to being alone, and honestly, I like it.

At the other end of spectrum we have the plain, old-fashioned desire to wait for the right relationship. More and more women are choosing to remain virgins late into their teens or throughout their early twenties, no longer feeling so intense a pressure to prove their sexual liberation. This has much to do ' living in the shadow of AIDS and other sexually transmitted

dern history, women are discov-

of sexual options.

men

soon be realized

will see that their sexual energy

and instrumental to creativity, health, and

shared with another or not. Indeed, it will seem increasing-,

ral and acceptable that a woman (or man) should have phases when sexual interaction is either inappropriate, undesirable, or low on the list of priorities, and that there will be times when sexual energy is channeled into highly personal pursuits.

1. Winnifred Cutler, *Love Cycles* (New York: Villard Books, 1991).

2. A. Moir and D. Jessel, *Brain Sex* (New York: Carol Publishing, 1991).

3. Barbara Walker, *The Crone* (San Francisco: Harper and Row, 1985).

H on th. . solved issues of a... affect your receptivity and sense of self tha. shadow natural changes at different stages of life.

And yet, as we live each day and notice the turning of each cycle, we also begin to observe certain things about ourselves, ways in which we remain troubled or inhibited: our toughest challenges. The more creatively and constructively we are able to work on these, the richer and more multidimensional our experience at the next stage will be.

This closing chapter is written workbook style, with specific questions intended to shed light on these psychosexual patterns. Rather than allow blank space for writing within the book, I encourage you to use separate paper. The questions are provocative and intimately revealing, and I doubt you would want someone browsing through your bookshelves to come across your responses.

But *do* write your answers down! Committing yourself in writing is altogether different from musing, even if aloud. As you write, you may notice certain words that keep cropping up, or phrases from the treasure box of your past that have deep and vivid meaning for you. Or you may find empty expressions that you might wish to rethink or change.

If you would like to evoke your personal sentiments more strongly, you might choose a colored pen that best represents your mood during a particular period and write with it. Or design a symbol—an open circle, a square cut in half, whatever—that summarizes your feelings at a certain stage, and place it at the top of each appropriate page. Your symbol can certainly change during a given cycle; you may well find that it does. If you have a tarot deck, select a card at critical junctures that embodies your feelings and beliefs, and make note of it. You may also change your name as you write, to a nickname or private "soul" name that no one knows but you.

The journey through the labyrinth of sexuality is not only personal, it is mythic. Don't be afraid to lend this dimension of value and significance to the intimate details of your life.

DISCOVERING YOUR CYCLE

If you are just now learning about your monthly cycle, certain questions and concerns will probably arise. Most women wonder why no one ever told them these facts about sex and their bodies before. Do you feel angry at having been kept in the dark this way? Or do you feel foolish or inept at never having noticed cyclic changes yourself? Does your formerly tranquil mind now reel with paranoia of plots and conspiracies against women in general? Or do you simply feel loss and sadness at having missed out on this aspect of yourself for some period of time? Quite commonly, women are both disturbed and exhilarated to think that romantic feelings attributed to a particular relationship or partner were in large part biological promptings coming from their own bodies at certain times of the month.

You may wish to go back through the questions in the previous paragraph and examine your feelings more closely. Explore them a bit in writing. See if you can get in touch with your history here, tracing back attitudes, inhibitions, and expectations. Go back to the beginning: how did you learn about menstruation? What was your menarche like—was it hidden from the rest of your family and friends, or acknowledged in some positive way? And how did you learn about sex? Were you given a chance to question? What were your initial explorations like? Do you remember the

first time you masturbated? How was it having sex the first time? How did you feel afterward? Balance the downside of any of these events by recalling the moments of power when you really felt ~~od about yourself. Evoke the curious, courageous you, unfettered ~onfidently following your destiny, and see this ' ~nd shouldn'ts you bear.
                                             '' ~nd bring it to the
                                                    ~''

It you .~ or can't deal with this at ..., checklist on sexual abuse.

If your cycle is basically smooth and trouble free, tan~ . ment to consider why. Do you follow any particular menstrual routine or ritual? Cultural mores see menstrual blood on a spectrum from dirty to sacred. How do you feel about it? Do you enjoy and make the most of your fertile time? How so? How do you benefit most from paying attention to your cycle? And what do you have yet to learn about honoring your rhythms?

If you are at the point of completing this sort of personal investigation, single out whatever aspects remain troublesome or unsettled for you. These are your carryover issues. As you move through other stages, you will come to see these problems in a different context, which may enable you to solve them.

PREGNANT FOR THE FIRST TIME

Having your first baby? Then you have much to contemplate, many emotional changes to enlighten and frighten you. You may have already discovered by now that pregnancy is definitely a social event. You are probably being bombarded with questions, advice, even physical contact (belly touching) from absolute strangers. This, you can't avoid. In fact, if you can stay somewhat open and objective, you may see in those encounters that affect you most deeply some fundamental bit of your conditioning that has been triggered.

Let's look at the background once again. What did your mother tell you about birth? How did you react? What about your grandmother, great-grandmother, or other female relatives? Try to recollect your *feelings* at these moments of revelation. Apart from any messages of fear or humiliation, if you were to summon each of these women now to stand before you, what sort of wisdom might each impart as to how to cope with labor?

Control is such an issue in pregnancy and birth. How do you personally feel about losing control? About feeling and appearing vulnerable? What do you think you might do if the pain really got to you? What sorts of things might your partner and midwife or doctor do to help you feel better? What might you do to help yourself? Do any of these relate to your sensual and sexual likes and dislikes?

Look at the last few questions, and see if there are things you might teach your partner or midwife now. For example, maybe you love to have your hair stroked, or your head held, only nobody knows but you. Pregnancy is the time to make these desires known—absolutely.

Fantasize about yourself in labor. Where are you? Is it dark, light, noisy, or quiet? Who is with you, and what are they doing? What are you doing? What position are you in, how are you breathing, and how do you feel?

Now imagine labor suddenly getting much stronger. Wow—it really hurts! How do you react? Do you expand, or contract? Do you reach out, or close yourself off? Relate this response to your experience with sex. What do you do when it stops feeling good, either emotionally or physically? Sometimes, women think they want to have sex even as they find themselves totally shutting down. Think about the times this has happened to you. Was it really sex you wanted, or something else? Crack the code on this, and you will discover the kind of support you are most likely to need in labor.

When you do feel sexually frustrated, how do you handle it? Do you ask for what you want, get angry, sulk, or just withdraw? In

every possible area of your life, especially in bed, practice asking
for what you need, when you need it. This is core preparation for
giving birth.

A little something more: how do you respond when others
···hat's good for you? Do you clam up, concede to
· ·nr assert your position? When it
·ine procedures you
¹ :ɔƖ·

Whether carrying your secu·
ably have issues remaining from your oui·i
merit attention. The central question is this: did you recι -
way violated during your birth experience? Were things done to
you or the baby that you did not desire or without your permission? Was your privacy invaded? Did you feel powerless, unsupported, ridiculed, or ridiculous in a way you can't let go of? Were
promises broken by your doctor or midwife? Do you feel they aban-
doned you during or after the birth?

If any of the above fit, you may want to write a letter to the
appropriate parties. Whether you send it or not, the writing is
therapeutic. You may not want to send the first draft, but may
decide to send the second. I personally think it is critical to let
your doctor or midwife know how you feel—critical for you, for
them, and for other women they serve.

How about your partner? Did he or she let you down or
disappoint you in any way? Do you have feelings about what happened during labor that you never shared? Did the birth affect your
sex life or intimacy? Again, a letter is a good place to start; it can
help you get your thoughts and feelings in order before you begin
to discuss them.

If your partner's behavior during the birth relates to some
preexisting problem that the two of you have already discussed
many times, you may be ripe for outside intervention via counsel-

ing. Perhaps you see the need, but can you assert it? If not, you yourself may be bound by some strong feelings of personal unworthiness. Perhaps you have a history of abuse. You need to find support and the opportunity to express your anxiety, either one to one with a counselor or in group therapy.

Do this work now; read and educate yourself on the option for giving birth, communicate your hopes and desires, and your next experience could be fundamentally different—the birth of your dreams!

NEWLY POSTPARTUM

If you are newly or recently postpartum, you may be encountering feelings of dependency. Often these arise during labor, although you may not have recognized them as such. Feelings of dependency are strongly linked to a fear of abandonment.

Let us not confuse dependency with vulnerability. Vulnerability is quite normal in labor and is actually a desired state. It is characterized by high levels of sensitivity, openness, and receptivity. Dependency, in contrast, is marked by feelings of not being able to rely on oneself, of needing others to define one's reality.

Actually, hospital policies and personnel often engender feelings of dependency in patients so that they will be compliant, even with the use of highly invasive, unnecessary procedures. But once a woman's power has thus been usurped, she may become desperately afraid that whoever has taken it will leave her behind and abandon her to the worst.

Here are some questions to help you see where you stand on this. Do you generally find it hard to focus on your own needs? Do you often feel that everyone else has power but you? Do you experience anxiety attacks when people pull away or reject you? These are actually behavioral characteristics of women who have suffered abuse, whether birth related or not. They also correlate to a family background of drug or alcohol dependency.

There is yet another category of abuse to consider: that perpetrated by society. In Chapter 4, we looked at the routine abandonment of new mothers in the United States. Even women who have led relatively stable lives may find themselves exhibiting typical dependency or fear of abandonment symptoms: anxiety and depression.

~~Women~~ can pull themselves out of this only with the support

~~family~~ members or other women. Generally,

~~practical~~ assistance with recov-

[1] support.

Perhaps

times there is a con...

traced back to rigid sex-role div...

affection in one's family. Was your mother long...

decidedly negative view of menstruation, childbearing, and se...

ity? If you are deeply uncomfortable about caring for your baby, frustration can build up and in extreme cases can lead to violence. Get help. Make an anonymous call to a women's hotline or counseling referral service.

We have discussed the typical sexual frustrations postpartum. Are you compounding these with negative feelings about your body? Do you find your copious secretions (milk, lochia, sweat) offensive? Do you feel ashamed that you look a bit softer or plumper than usual? Or can you take pride in your body for all it has accomplished, birth and breastfeeding and day-to-day recovery, along with care of the newborn baby?

Has your weight been an issue for most of your adult life? If so, you will probably be somewhat unhappy postpartum. Have you a history of eating disorders? Nothing is worse than trying to diet while breastfeeding; in fact, you need more calories than you did while pregnant. Exercise is the answer, even though it takes a while to get used to going out with the baby in a sling, or to find the energy and time for an exercise video while the baby naps.

Other considerations: do you feel conflict between being a mother and being sexual? Where does this come from? What are your partner's attitudes on this subject? It may seem awkward to switch back and forth between erotic and maternal feelings as abruptly as you do at this stage, but eventually they will find their place in your life.

What it all comes down to is this: can you give yourself permission to change and grow? Your body is changing—can you trust it to tell you what to eat and drink, trust that it will fully recover in good time, trust that its promptings for rest are to be heeded? Or do you feel that your body has somehow betrayed you? Have others told you outright that your body is not up to par, not good enough? Think of every individual who has told you this throughout the years, and explore your respective feelings. Can you let go of your anger and find forgiveness?

Keep a journal of your daily accomplishments at this stage, noting in particular every way in which your body works for you. Pay special attention to the times you feel physically well and wonderful, and write them down.

JUGGLING CAREER, FAMILY, AND INTIMACY

The work to be done in this area can probably be summed up in a single question: what are your priorities? Often, we learn more about our values if we examine the priorities of our parents. Are we emulating them, reacting against what they believe, or truly on our own?

Ever since the 1950s, women have typically attempted to do too much. How was it in your household? What were the messages you got from your mother regarding housework? Responsibility for children? Responsibility for emotional issues? Responsibility for individual health and well-being?

What was your mother's attitude regarding her privacy? Did she take private time? What were the things she loved to do—just for herself? Did she set boundaries that you and other family members were aware of and respected?

Generally, women tend to make care of their children a top priority, and that is as it should be. But did your mother have any help? What kind and how often? Do you think it was enough?

This brings us to the subjects of stress and anger. How did your mother handle each of these? How do you handle each of these? And how does what you do, or don't do, affect you and your loved ones?

What was your parents' attitude about their intimate rela-

··········· ·heir romantic feelings for one another

·········· ·apart from you? How

······· ·l ···rge

fit from writing dow..

of time spent in each general area: care..,

action, personal pursuits, and private time with your pai u..

with this on paper, look at any gross imbalance, and reallocate your time according to what you really want. Many of us believe we are trapped in unsatisfactory lifestyle patterns by necessity, when in fact these are a matter of habit. What every woman in this stage of life needs to recognize is that there will *never* be enough time to do and have it all. Instead, the source of self-satisfaction can change from week to week and month to month, depending on any urgent needs. Dial and tune your reality, and resolve to stop being a victim.

If this seems extremely difficult for you, look back at your family history and your responses to the questions in previous sections of this chapter. What are the patterns? Perhaps if you can see where and when you give up your power, you will be able to figure out why.

PASSING THROUGH MENOPAUSE

As was mentioned in Chapter 6, your responses in this phase are likely to reflect those of female relatives and particularly your mother. What did she experience at menopause? Is there anything of her experience that you personally remember? Since most women tend to hide these changes, you may want to ask her about any erratic behavior you recall and see what the two of you can piece together.

Moving to yet another area: how do you feel about the passing of youth? Do you believe that youth is merely a state of mind, one that can be maintained indefinitely? If so, what are you doing to keep yourself young and vital? Are you keeping up with your interests? How about your spiritual life?

And how are you caring for your body at this point? Take inventory of all current measures you are taking to try to stay physically youthful and attractive. Truthfully, are any of these a waste of time and money? What does seem to work for you, and can you place greater priority on it?

Have you talked to your partner about your fears and anxieties at this point in your life? Has she or he been supportive? As the hormonal surges of menopause move you deeper and closer to your deepest concerns and longings, do you find yourself able to utilize these visions? Are you incorporating them into your life, or merely coping?

Begin to think about where you want to go with the energy of "the change." Use it as a springboard to shift and expand your lifestyle. Where do you find courage in general, and where can you find it most right now?

GROWING OLDER AND WISER

How do you feel about growing older? What do you still look forward to doing and accomplishing? And how about your partner? Have you discussed your rounding-out goals and dreams with one another?

What, if any, are the lessons you have yet to learn in life? About the situations that keep repeating themselves? And what will it take for you to move through them? Can you deliberately set the stage? To what degree are you willing to do this? In terms of these, your toughest challenges, what is your source of strength for confronting them, and how do you get to that source?

With regard to sex: how is your communication with your partner? Are you happy with yourself sexually? More or less than before? In terms of sexual expression, are there things you would still like to try and do? How do you think your partner would feel

1:d so?

' '--l- back. What, if any, are the ways you

' '--? The parts you never

--over

you comfortable sha......

Identify your crone/destroyer aspect: w..,

bly frank. When the crone speaks, she does so from u ,

clarity and certitude. Feel the difference in tone between whining or cajoling and speaking the truth, unfettered by expectation.

Do you have other outlets for your accumulated wisdom? Can you find any more? Your vitality is strongly linked to this fundamental sort of self-expression.

Have you considered taking the role of family historian? Perhaps, if you have not done so already, you might begin to assemble and organize papers and photographs into albums, adding your own narrative if you like. Each of your children may have his or her own album, and there may be a more general one that includes the family tree. These will be treasured by your offspring and will put much into perspective for you while bringing to a close certain periods of your life.

IN SUMMARY

Now that you have had a chance to work on each phase of life you have already experienced, and have read about others yet to come, perhaps you have begun to see some underlying themes of family history, cultural conditioning, self-discovery, and ultimately, transcendence. For beyond self-realization and integration, the transcendental aspect of sexual expression is what keeps us coming back for more. As Andrew Weil has pointed out in his book *The Natural Mind,* the desire for altered states of reality is with us from the time we are very young: why else do children spin wildly in circles until they fall down dizzy and laughing, only to get up and do it again? It becomes a bit more difficult to find appropriate ways to do this as we mature, but that doesn't mean we shouldn't go on trying!

As women, our journey through this particular period of history is tremendously rich and complex. Having an overview of the cycles and stages in life can help us keep our wits about us, retain our sense of humor, and become wise. Even now, the men's movement is becoming better defined and likewise seeks a complete view of what it means to be male: personally, interpersonally, and socially. Never has it been more important, or in many ways easier, to articulate all that it means to be female.

Nevertheless, way too many women live in poverty, abusive situations, or other conditions of hardship for us to become complacent. We have so much to do, so much to speak and write about, so much to share across the generations. May our sexual vitality and sensitivity infuse these tasks with passion, commitment, and love. And may we readily find courage at every crossroads.

Index

A

abortion, 11, 42, 56

abstinence, physical effects of, 181
  sexual, 175–185

abuse, emotional, 161–171
  profiles of, 163–171

abuse, physical, 154–160

abuse, signs of early, 156–157

acupuncture, 34, 49

addiction, sexual, 171–173

adhesions, endometriosis, 42

adolescence, 116

adrenal glands, 26

adrenaline, 75, 85, 109

aerobic exercise, 37

aging, 196–197

AIDS, 185

alcohol, 42, 45, 124, 137

amenorrhea, 42

androgens, 29, 33, 109

anesthesia, during birth, 78

anger, 108–109

B

backache, 6, 181

barrier methods, contraception,
  51–53

basil, 44, 49

bioflavenoids, 131, 132

biological gender differences, 16,
  18–19, 179

biological rhythms, 16, 18–19, 45

birth, environmental factors, 72
  home, 72–73

bisexuality, 121

black cohosh root, 49, 132, 134

black currant, 49

black haw, 132

bleeding, 124

excess, 132
  after childbirth, 91, 93
  breakthrough, 34, 47
  during pregnancy, 59
  hysterectomy, 141–142
  menopause, 132
  Pill users, 34, 47

blue cohosh, 49

bonding, mother and child, 88

bone mass, loss of, 134–136

breathing, during labor, 76–77

breast cancer, 128

breastfeeding, 84–85, 89

breasts, 29, 58

Buddhist tradition, 146

C

caffeine, 130, 137

calcium citrate, 135

calcium, 135

cancer, 131
  breast, 128
  uterine, 124, 128

catecholamines, 109

catnip, 44, 132

cayenne pepper, 132

celibacy, 175–185

cervical cap, 3, 51–52

cervix, 27
  after childbirth, 90
  during pregnancy, 56
  endometriosis, 42
  labor, 67–68, 70, 71, 74
  mucus, 27

cesarean birth, 73

chaste tree (vitex), 49

chemical dependency, 108

child rearing, 3

childbearing, 3

tearing 78
vaginal stimulation and bonding, 77
vaginismus, 158–159
valerian root, 132
vegetables, 136
virginity, 199
vitamin A, 132
vitamin C, 124, 132
vitamin D, 132, 134
vitamin E, 132, 133
vitex, 132

W

water retention, 29
weight changes, 29
whole grains, 136
wild yam root, 49, 132
women's groups, 150, 180–181
workload, 195

Y

yeast infections, 52, 128

Z

zinc, 132

SEXUAL PLEASURE: Reaching New Heights of Sexual Arousal and Intimacy by Barbara Keesling, Ph.D.

This bestselling book is for all people who are interested in enhancing their sex lives and experiencing lovemaking as a deeply pleasurable physical and emotional exchange. Written ... . encouraging tone, it helps readers to recognize the .... of their own sensuality

intense levels of arousal, ...
Special chapter include ways to make sex playful and ....
for working with the differences between male and female arousal. The open and loving approach of the book is conveyed artistically in the tasteful, sensual photographs that complement the text, making it the perfect gift for caring partners.

224 pages ... 14 illus. ... Paperback $12.95 ... Hard cover $21.95

SEXUAL HEALING: A Self-help Program to Enhance Your Sensuality and Overcome Common Sexual Problems by Barbara Keesling, Ph.D.

Using her experience as both a surrogate partner and a sex therapist, Dr. Keesling gives individuals and couples expert advice on how to overcome common sexual problems in the comfort and security of their own home. She offers specific techniques to effectively eliminate problems such as performance anxiety, premature ejaculation, erection problems, low desire issues, and inability to achieve orgasm.

The basis of the exercises is sensate focus —touching for your own pleasure, keeping your mind on the moment, and focusing on the exact point of touch. These proven techniques have worked on thousands of clients.

288 pages ... Paperback ... $12.95

Barbara Keesling, Ph.D., is a sex therapist and was a surrogate partner for more than twelve years. She has a doctorate in psychology from the University of California and has appeared on "Real Personal," "The Howard Stern Show" and in Playboy and Cosmopolitan.

To order please see last page or call (800) 266-5592

ORDER FORM

10% DISCOUNT on orders of $50 or more —
20% DISCOUNT on orders of $150 or more —
30% DISCOUNT on orders of $500 or more —
On cost of books for fully prepaid orders

NAME

ADDRESS

CITY/STATE   ZIP/POSTAL CODE

PHONE   COUNTRY (outside U.S.A.)

TITLE	QTY	PRICE	TOTAL
Women, Sex & Desire (paperback)		@ $12.95	
Women, Sex & Desire (hard cover)		@ $22.95	
Special: **All 3 A-to-Z books** *(paperback)*		**@ $34.95**	
Please list other titles below:			
		@ $	
		@ $	
		@ $	
		@ $	
		@ $	
		@ $	
		@ $	
		@ $	

Shipping costs:
*First book: $2.50
($6.00 outside U.S.)
Each additional book:
$.75 ($3.00 outside
U.S.)
For UPS rates and
bulk orders call us at
(510) 865-5282*

TOTAL _____

Less discount @ _____%   (_____)
TOTAL COST OF BOOKS _____
Calif. residents add sales tax _____
Shipping & handling _____
TOTAL ENCLOSED _____
Please pay in U.S. funds only

❏ Check   ❏ Money Order   ❏ Visa   ❏ M/C   ❏ Discover

Card # _____ Exp date _____

Signature _____

Complete and mail to:

Hunter House Inc., Publishers
PO Box 2914, Alameda CA 94501-0914
Orders: 1-800-266-5592
Phone (510) 865-5282 Fax (510) 865-4295
❏ Check here to receive our book catalog

WSX 8/95